THE SPECTRUM OF
MUSIC

with Related Arts

Illustrated by
Errol LeCain
John Gamache
Sal Murdooca
Chris Notarile
David Palladini
Bob Pepper
Dave Roe
William Woods

Photos by
Alfred Fisher
Norman Snyder
Cover Design by Thomas Upshur

THE SPECTRUM OF

MUSIC

with Related Arts

A Macmillan/Schirmer program

Mary Val Marsh
Carroll Rinehart
Edith Savage

Macmillan Publishing Co., Inc.
New York

Collier Macmillan Publishers
London

ACKNOWLEDGMENTS

Grateful acknowledgment is given to the following authors and publishers:

Antioch Press for "On Watching the Construction of a Skyscraper" by Burton Raffel. Reprinted from THE ANTIOCH REVIEW, vol. XX, no. 4, by permission of the editors.

Associated Music Publishers Inc. and Lorenz Publishing Company for "A Song of Peace." Used by permission.

Belwin Mills Publishing Corp. for "Scarborough Fair" from THE SINGING ISLAND by Seeger and MacColl, used by permission; and for "Carol of the Drums" by Katherine Davis Copyright © 1941, © 1969 Mills Music Inc.; and for "Tzena, Tzena" by Parish, Miron, and Grossman. Copyright 1950 by Mills Music, Inc. Used with permission. All rights reserved.

Bill Brohn for the music of "Fender Bender" and "Listen Inside the Sound," words by George Guilbault. Used by permission.

Clara Music Publishing Corp. for "Island in the Sun" by Harry Belafonte and Lord Burgess. © Copyright 1956 by Clara Music Corp. All Rights Reserved. Used by permission.

Cooperative Recreation Service, Inc. for "We Shall Overcome" from ONE IN SONG, "Let Us Sing Together," "Rock-a-My Soul," "Music Alone Shall Live," and "Sing Together" from 101 ROUNDS, "Golden Slumbers" and "Kuma Echa" from WORK AND SING, "Sakura" from JAPANESE SONGS, "Harvesters" from SECOND PROOF BOOK, "Worried Man Blues," "Amen," "Sun Ah Go Down," and "Holla Hi, Holla Ho" from JOYFUL SINGING, "Morning Song" (Las Mañanitas) from GOLDEN BRIDGES, "Oh, I Remember" from PEOPLES OF EARTH, and "Vreneli." Used by permission.

Doubleday & Company, Inc. for "The Snake" from AN INTRODUCTION TO HAIKU by Harold Henderson. Copyright © 1958 by Harold G. Henderson. Reprinted by permission of Doubleday & Company, Inc.

Editions Durand & Cie for "Tenez La de Pres" (Hold Tight to Your Girl) from FOLK SONGS OF FRANCE. Copyright © 1966. Used by permission.

David Ernst for "Rondo." Used by permission.

Fideree Music for "Wo Ye Le." Words & Music by Josef Marais (ASCAP). Copyright 1960 Fideree Music. Used by permission.

Follett Educational Corporation for "Come and Sing Together," translated by Max T. Krone, from DISCOVERING MUSIC TOGETHER by Leonard et al. Reprinted by permission.

Girl Scouts of the U.S.A. for "A Song of the Open Air" from THE DITTY BAG by Janet E. Tobitt. Used by permission of the author.

Alfred A. Knopf for "Dream Variation." Copyright 1926 by Alfred A. Knopf, Inc., renewed 1954 by Langston Hughes. From SELECTED POEMS, by Langston Hughes. Reprinted by permission of the publisher.

Parts of this work were published in earlier editions of *The Spectrum of Music with Related Arts.*

Macmillan Publishing Co., Inc.
866 Third Avenue, New York, New York 10022
Collier Macmillan Canada, Inc.

Printed in the United States of America
ISBN 0-02-291960-0
9 8 7 6 5 4

Mrs. George Korson for "Joe Magarac" from PENNSYL-VANIA SONGS AND LEGENDS by George Korson, John Hopkins edition, 1960.

Mark VII Music for "Sing a Rainbow" by Arthur Hamilton.

E.B. Marks Music Corp. for "Song of the Islands." Copyright Edward B. Marks Music Corporation. Used by permission.

David McKay Co., Inc. for "Sing! Sing! Sing!" adapted from ECHOES OF AFRICA IN FOLK SONGS OF THE AMERICAS by Beatrice Landeck, second revised edition. Copyright © 1961, 1969 by Beatrice Landeck. Used by permission of David McKay Co., Inc.

Music Sales Corporation for "I've Been to Gather Mussels" from FOLK SONGS OF FRANCE — compiled and edited by Barbara Scott. © 1966 Oak Publications. Used by Permission. For "Crawdad" ("The Crawdad Song") from AMERICAN FAVORITE BALLADS by Pete Seeger © 1961 Oak Publications. Used by Permission.

Harold Ober Associates. Reprinted by permission. Copyright 1951 by Eleanor Farjeon. "The Night Will Never Stay" from ELEANOR FARJEON'S POEMS FOR CHILDREN. Copyright 1951 by Eleanor Farjeon. By permission of J. B. Lippincott, Publishers.

Ronald Lo Presti for "Snakes." Used by permission.

Henry T. Rockwell for "City Nights" by James Flexner from CREATIVE YOUTH by Hugh Mearns. Used by permission.

G. Schirmer, Inc. for "Marching to Pretoria" by Joseph Marais from SONGS FROM THE VELD, published 1942. Used by permission.

G. Schirmer, Inc. for "The Shepherd Boy" Greek folksong translated by Aristides E. Phoutrides. From BOTS-FORD COLLECTION OF FOLKSONGS, Vol. 3 by Florence H. Botsford, published 1933. Used by permission.

Schroder Music Co. (ASCAP) for "In Bethlehem" words and music by Malvina Reynolds © Copyright 1960 by Schroder Music Co. (ASCAP). Used by permission.

Simon and Schuster, Inc. for "The Ol' Gray Goose" from FIRESIDE BOOK OF FAVORITE AMERICAN SONGS by Margaret B. Boni. Copyright © 1952 by Simon and Schuster, Inc. and Artist and Writers Guild, Inc. Reprinted by permission.

Stormking for TALKING BLUES ("Original Talking Blues") By Lee Hays, Fred Hellerman and Ronnie Gilbert © Copyright 1958 by SANGA MUSIC INC. All rights reserved. Used by Permission. For NEW YORK CITY By Joe Jaffe, Irwin Silber, Gladys Bashkin and Ernie Lieberman © Copyright 1948 by STORMKING MUSIC INC. All rights reserved. Used by permission.

Walton Music Corp. for "Beyond the Mountain" from SONGS OF MAN by Norman Luboff. Used by permission.

David Ward-Steinman for "The Web" by David Ward-Steinman and Susan Lucas. Used by permission.

AUTHORS

Mary Val Marsh has been a member of the Music Education faculty of San Diego State University and is well known as a workshop clinician. She has had extensive experience teaching and supervising classroom music at every level from kindergarten through graduate school and is the author of *Choruses and Carols, Here a Song, There a Song,* and *Explore and Discover Music.*

Carroll A. Rinehart has been Coordinator of Elementary music and a principal of an alternative open-education school in the Tucson, Arizona, Unified School District. He has served as a consultant and workshop clinician on the Manhattanville Music Curriculum Project. He is author of five choral collections.

Edith J. Savage, Professor of Music, San Diego State University, has taught and supervised classroom teachers of music at every level from kindergarten through graduate school. She is the co-author of *Teaching Children to Sing,* and co-author of *First Experience in Music,* a college text for elementary teachers.

CONSULTANTS

William Brohn, consultant in rock and popular music, is a conductor, performer, and arranger in New York City.

Venoris Cates, consultant in Afro-American music, is a music supervisor in the Chicago Public Schools and has had long experience teaching music in elementary schools.

Wayne Johnson, musicology consultant, is Chairman of the Department of Music, Georgetown College, Georgetown, Ky.

Walter E. Purdy, consultant in music education, is Coordinator of Music Education, University of Houston.

John Rouillard, consultant in American Indian music, is a member of a Sioux tribe. He is in charge of the program of Indian studies, San Diego State University.

Jose Villarino, consultant in Mexican-American music, is an Assistant Professor of Mexican-American studies, San Diego State University.

David L. Wilmot, general consultant on the Teacher's Annotated Edition, is a Professor of Music Education, University of Florida at Gainesville.

Contents

RELATED ARTS

Works of Art

"Twittering Machine," Paul Klee, 56
"Light Tube Sculpture,"
  Stephen Antonakos, 61
"Zapatistas," José Clemente Orozco, 62
"The Green Violinist," Marc Chagall, 76
"Sympan," Michael Lekakis, 81
Horyuji Temple (Nara Japan), 103
"Woman with Scroll," Toyonobu, 105
"Composition in a Square,"
  Piet Mondrian, 107
"The Bride," Henry Moore, 114

"Sanctuary," Seymour Lipton, 128
"Autumn Rhythm," Jackson Pollock, 130
"La Mer au Havre," Raoul Dufy, 136
"Still Life with Three Puppies,"
  Paul Gauguin, 143
"Automatic Drawing," Jean Arp, 145

Art Activities

Photography, 67
Painting with brush and watercolors, 105
Paper compositions, 107
Making sculpture with contrast, 114

Linda Lindroth

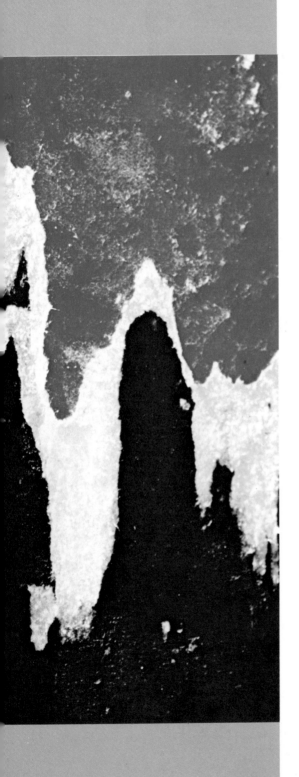

The media of music

In music, the word media means "sound sources." If you were to write down all of the sound sources you know, your list might be quite long. Composers and instrument makers are always experimenting to find ways of producing new sounds. The new sounds make much of the music of today very exciting.

Music is being written not only for human voices and orchestral instruments, but also for electronic instruments, folk instruments, and for many instruments borrowed from other cultures.

The 20th century artist often creates with tools and materials that are very different from those used by artists working in earlier times. Traditional media such as paint and clay are still being used, but there are many artists who have used media usually associated with technology: metals, plastics, electricity, and even computers.

The sound of rock

This is a popular rock group. All of the members of this group are good musicians. Some of them studied music in school, and some taught themselves. Name the instruments in the picture that you know.

What makes rock music so popular? Probably the main reasons for its popularity are the media used in rock — instruments and voices — and the strong rhythm. Rock music can be played on almost any musical instrument. Its strong metric beat makes it easy for anyone who sings or plays an instrument to join in. The instruments first used in rock music were electric guitars and drums, and voices. These same instruments are used by most rock groups today.

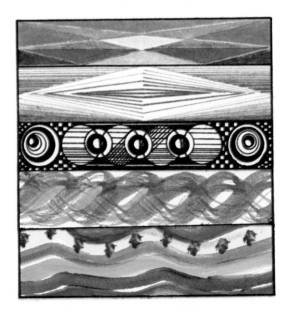

You will be able to use art media more effectively by becoming familiar with their characteristics. Drawing media have different properties which affect the way they produce dark-light and dull-bright qualities.

Artists sometimes use tools that are not usually associated with drawing or painting. Straws, twigs, and cotton swabs may also be used as tools. Paint a picture without using brushes. Use only tools not normally connected with painting. Be imaginative, and discover the many different effects you can create.

Listen to "Fender Bender." A "fender bender" is a bass guitar player. The melody in "Fender Bender" is played on an electric guitar. Compare the sounds of this guitar with those of the bass guitar. The sound of the bass guitar will be easy to recognize because it plays alone for two measures.

Fender Bender

Music by Bill Brohn
Words by George Guilbault

Fen - der ben - der, yea, yea, yea!__

Play,__ play,__ play, yea, yea, yea!__ Play that rhy - thm,

yea, yea, yea!__ All the way,____ yea, yea, yea!__

Bend that beat__ a - round syn - co - pa - tion sound! Fen - der ben - der,

yea, yea, yea!__ All the way,____ yea, yea, yea!__

Yea, yea, yea!__ Yea, yea, yea!__

Rock songs performed at a high volume level and with a steady, driving beat are examples of "hard rock." The sound is exciting.

"Listen Inside the Sound" is a folk rock song and has a gentle, flowing feeling. Folk rock has a slower tempo and is quieter than hard rock. Listen for the sounds of the electronic organ, and identify some of the other instruments you hear on the recording.

Listen Inside the Sound

Music by Bill Brohn
Words by George Guilbault

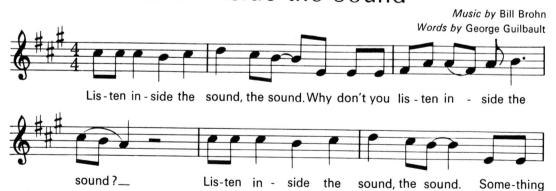

Lis-ten in-side the sound, the sound. Why don't you lis-ten in - side the sound?__ Lis-ten in - side the sound, the sound. Some-thing

won-der-ful __ can be found. __ Some-thing won-der-ful __ can be

Fine

found ! In-side the sound there's love for your fel-low man.

In - side the sound there's hope for a bet-ter plan.

In - side, __ a spe-cial dream. In - side, __ a

D.C. al Fine

whole new scheme. In - side ! _____

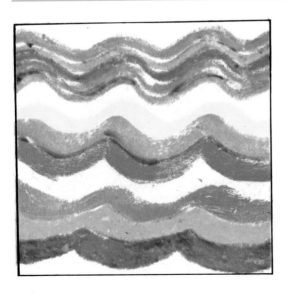

Another drawing medium is crayon. There are various types of crayon, each with its own characteristics. Pastels are made by mixing chalk with pigments. When oil is added to the chalk, oil pastels are produced. But wax crayons are the most common. In ancient Roman days, artists made astonishingly realistic pictures by painting with melted colored wax. Make a picture, using watercolors and crayons. Afterwards, go over the paper with a hot iron, first placing a sheet of paper over your picture. This will melt the wax and alter the picture, softening the lines and intensifying the colors.

Percussion instruments in rock

Everyone likes to see and hear the drummer in a rock group. Rock drummers usually have several instruments. They have a snare drum, two or more deeper drums, a bass drum, and several sets of cymbals.

Drummers are exciting to watch because they often are so busy. Drummers use their hands and feet all the time. Moving from drum to cymbal and back to drum, they can create many different rhythms and timbres at the same time. These all fit into the song, over the basic beat.

Alfred Fisher

The rhythm of rock is different from the rhythm of other kinds of music. It is almost impossible to listen to rock rhythm without responding to the music in some way, whether it is by clapping your hands, tapping your feet, or dancing.

The meter of rock is often **duple.** This means that there are two or four metric beats in each measure. The metric beat is often played loudly on the drums.

Here are some background rhythms that are often heard in rock music.

Play these rhythms on percussion instruments. Then find these or other rhythms in a rock recording; clap or play them while you listen. This will help you feel the rhythm of rock.

Rock music began in the early 1950's. It grew from a merging of popular ballads, rhythm and blues, country western music, and jazz. An early popular recording of rock and roll music was "Shake, Rattle, and Roll" by Bill Haley and his Comets. Elvis Presley then made his famous recordings of "Blue Suede Shoes" and "You Ain't Nothin' But a Hound Dog."

Rock music has changed very much since its beginning. The guitar, drums, and the strong beat have remained, but many other kinds of music and instruments have been incorporated into rock music. In the early 1960's the Beatles brought to rock music new ideas and a fresh outlook. They used instruments from other countries, such as the sitar from India. Their style influenced many other rock groups. Structures and scales found in music from other countries became a part of some types of rock. Combinations of rock and other kinds of music appeared—jazz rock, folk rock, "billy rock," and soul music.

Rock music changes from day to day. The best way to learn about rock music is to listen to a different rock piece each week.

Handmade rock instruments

You can make your own drums and other percussion instruments that are used with rock music. Use nail kegs, heavy cartons, pieces of pipe, or small boxes with a few dried beans or buttons inside. You may want to build the following instruments.

HANDMADE DRUMS

A heavy wooden nail keg makes a sturdy drum. Take the top and bottom out of the keg. Stretch heavy plastic or rubber sheeting over the top and bottom of the keg; nail or staple the sheeting securely around the edges. Muslin cloth can also be used. Apply spray starch to the cloth after it is stretched and fastened in place.

Drums can also be made from large ice cream cartons and coffee cans of various sizes. A plastic lid makes a good drumhead. Use a pencil, a drumstick, or your hand for a beater.

WIND CHIMES

Collect various sizes of nails, scraps of metal, pieces of pottery, strips of wood, dowels, or pieces of bamboo. Tie a piece of string to each item. Tie the strings to a straight bar, or hang them from a circular band made of flexible metal stripping, a small box lid, or a circle cut from a pegboard. Hang the pieces so they move freely and strike one another when they move. The instrument you construct will produce some very interesting sounds.

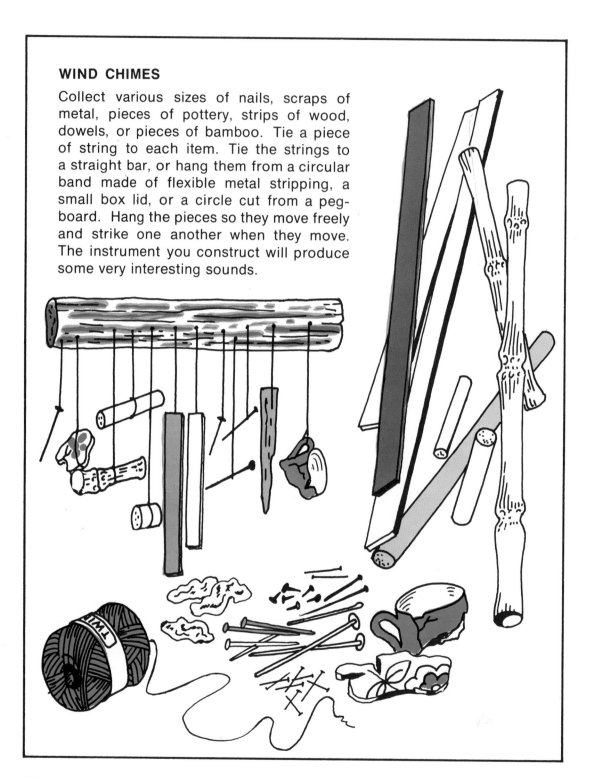

MARACAS

Maracas and other kinds of rattles are often used in rock music. You can make similar instruments. Use salt boxes, half-pound coffee cans, or any other small containers that can be sealed easily. Fill the containers with a handful of dried beans or corn, buttons, rice, or small stones. You can use a piece of doweling to make a handle.

Play your own instruments or standard percussion instruments as a background for the song "Fender Bender." First play the rhythms on page 9. Then make up other rhythm patterns that fit this music.

Drums of the world

Drums have been important in man's life since the beginning of civilization. The first drums were probably hollowed-out logs, slit on one side. Such drums are still used in some parts of the world.

Drums come in all sizes. They can be played with mallets or with the fingers. Listen to this example of expert drumming. It is a part of a drum improvisation by Jon Szanto.

Improvisation No. 2 for Percussion
Jon Szanto

Drums which are used in bands and orchestras are constructed in one of three different ways.

1. One drumhead is stretched over a frame. The frame is open at the bottom. The bongo and the conga drums are built in this way. Bongo and conga drums are played with Latin-American music.

Rhythm Band, Inc.

2. Two drumheads are stretched over both ends of a cylindrical frame. The bass and snare drums are examples of this type of drum. Bass and snare drums are played in marching bands, concert bands, jazz and dance bands, orchestras, and rock groups.

Courtesy of Ludwig Industries, Chicago.

15

3. One drumhead is stretched over the top of a kettle-shaped frame. Timpani, also called kettledrums, are made in this way. Usually two, three, or four timpani are played in a performance. Timpani can be tuned to definite pitches. They are the most important drums in the symphony orchestra and concert band.

One of the most unusual drums is the talking drum of Africa. Its African name is *bintin obonu*. Its flexible head makes it possible to play both high and low sounds. A skillful drummer can make these sounds rise and fall like a speaking voice. Messages sent on a talking drum can be heard and understood by people far away. Travelers in Africa have been astonished to find that the villagers have known they were coming long before they arrived, even though there were no telephones, telegraph wires, or radios. News of their approach was relayed from village to village by the *bintin obonu*.

Drum Talk
Danlee Mitchell

"Drum Talk" is music in which only drums and voices are heard. You will hear conversations between the singers and African talking drums. Try to guess what they are saying.

The carved drum in the photograph above was made by an artist of the Yoruba tribe of Nigeria, a country in west Africa. Although a variety of designs is used, all of the sections of the drum are unified. How did the artist achieve unity?

The other drum was made in Uganda, a country in central Africa. The skin of this drumhead is tied down with grass twine. Notice the curved line near the base of the drum created by the grass twine. This curved line complements the roundness of the drum.

17

"Wo Ye Le" is a song taken from the chant of African canoe paddlers on Lake Tanganyika. Use these patterns to accompany the song on the drums.

Wo Ye Le

Canoers' Chant
Arranged by Josef Marais

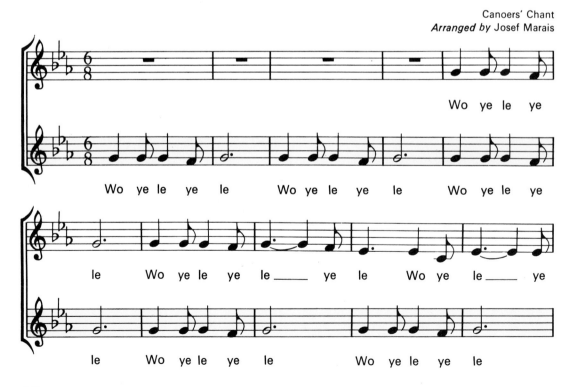

"Carol of the Drum" is a song of our own day that has become a popular Christmas carol.

Carol of the Drum

Words and music by Katherine K. Davis

Come, they told me,
Ba - by Je - sus,
Pa - rum-pa-pum - pum, _____

Our new-born King to see,
I'm _____ a poor boy too,
Pa - rum-pa-pum - pum, _____

Our fin - est gifts we'll bring,
I have no gift to bring,
Pa - rum-pa-pum - pum, _____

To lay be - fore the King!
That's fit to give a King,
Pa - rum-pa-pum-pum, Rum-pa-pum-pum,

Rum-pa - pum - pum, _____
So to hon - or Him,
Shall I play for you,
Pa-

rum - pa - pum - pum, _____

When_ we come._____
On ___ my drum?_____

Ma - ry nod - ded, Pa - rum - pa - pum - pum, _____

The ox and lamb kept time, Pa - rum - pa - pum - pum, _____

I played my drum for Him, Pa - rum - pa - pum - pum, _____

I played my best for Him, Pa - rum - pa - pum - pum, Rum - pa - pum - pum,

Rum - pa - pum - pum, _____

Then He smiled at me, Pa - rum - pa - pum - pum! ____

p *pp* *ppp*

Me and my drum! _____
(Sustain on "mmmm")

The guitar and its cousins

You have often heard the guitar played as an accompaniment for folk singing or as an important instrument in a rock group. The guitar is also used as a solo instrument to perform folk music and to play the music written for it by great composers.

The guitar is a member of a large family of stringed instruments that are played by plucking or strumming. The instruments in the guitar family have certain things in common. The strings are stretched over a **body** and **neck**. The neck is fitted with a **finger board**. Most instruments of the guitar family have **frets** attached to the finger board. Frets are small bars of metal or other material which show the player where to place his fingers to obtain the desired pitches. Frets also give the tone a sharp, clear sound.

Several kinds of guitars are used today, and there are several ways of playing them. The most familiar type of guitar is called the "Spanish" or "classical" guitar. This type of guitar is also called the "acoustic" guitar to distinguish it from the electric guitar. The term "acoustic" means that it produces its own sounds, while the tone of the electric guitar is controlled by amplifiers.

LISTENING *Verdad*
Flamenco Guitar

The method of playing the guitar varies according to the type of music being performed. Listen to the **flamenco** music on the recording. Flamenco music is a brilliant and colorful blend of Spanish and gypsy dance music.

Courtesy of The Art Institute of Chicago, The Helen Birch Bartlett Memorial.

The great artist Pablo Picasso created this painting when he was 22 years old. In it he shows his concern for the suffering of people, the subject of many of his works. Picasso used very somber warm and cool grays, blues and black. The old man appears to be part of the guitar, and the angular lines in his body are in strong contrast to the soft curves of the guitar. This contrast adds both interest and power to the painting.

The Cowboy

From THE COWBOY SINGS by Kenneth S. Clark, "The Cowboy" by F. W. Chamberlin. Used by permission of Shawnee Press, Inc.

The guitar is played in a special way in Hawaiian music. The player slides a bar up and down the strings of the instrument. This gives a slurring effect, or glissando, which is well-suited to the slow, dreamy melodies of Hawaii.

Song of the Islands

Words and music by Charles E. King

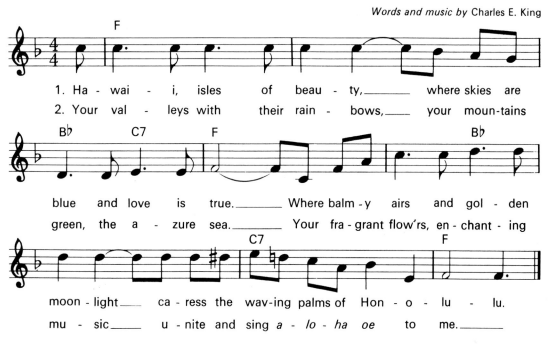

1. Ha - wai - i, isles of beau - ty,_____ where skies are
2. Your val - leys with their rain - bows,____ your moun-tains

blue and love is true._____ Where balm - y airs and gol - den
green, the a - zure sea._____ Your fra - grant flow'rs, en - chant - ing

moon - light____ ca - ress the wav-ing palms of Hon - o - lu - lu.
mu - sic_____ u - nite and sing *a - lo - ha oe* to me.____

The lute

The **lute** is closely related to the guitar. Like the guitar, the lute has a fretted neck and is plucked. The back of the lute, however, is rounded, while the guitar has a flat back. The lute is an ancient instrument. Lute-like instruments were played as early as 2000 B.C.

Lately there has been a new interest in the lute, probably because it is such an appropriate instrument for accompanying folk singing. Before you sing "Greensleeves," listen to the lute on the recording.

National Gallery, London.

This picture was painted during the Renaissance, over 500 years ago. The artist used a medium called tempera to paint on a wooden panel. Tempera is made by mixing colored pigments with the yolk of an egg, which acts as a glue for sticking colors to the wood. It was a favorite medium during the Renaissance.

Make tempera by mixing an egg yolk with powdered paint. Thin the mixture with water. Paint a picture on cardboard with your tempera. Tempera dries in minutes, and the colors lighten considerably.

Greensleeves

16th Century English Song

A - las,   my love,___ you do   me wrong___ to   cast   me off ____ dis-

cour - teous-ly;   And   I   have loved _____ you   so   long,___ De-

light - ing   in _____ your   com - pa - ny.

Green - sleeves_____ was   all   my   joy,_____

Green - sleeves _____ was   my   de - light.

Green - sleeves   was   my   heart   of   gold, _____ And

who,   but   my   la - dy   Green - sleeves.

The banjo

The **banjo** is another stringed instrument that is often used to accompany folk singing. Its body consists of a piece of calfskin or parchment attached to a circular metal frame. A wooden sounding board may be attached to the back, or the back may be left open. The twangy sound of the banjo is easy to recognize. The banjo player uses a rapid, vigorous strum.

Ring, Ring the Banjo

Words and music by Stephen C. Foster
Words Adapted

The beau-ties of cre - a - tion will nev - er lose their
Oh, nev - er count the bub - bles while there's wa - ter in the

charm, While I roam the old plan - ta - tion with my
spring, You'll__ nev - er meet with trou - bles if you've

1. **2.**

true love on my arm.
got this song to sing.

Ring, ring the ban - jo! I like that good old song;

Come a - gain, my true love, Oh, where you been so long?

Other stringed instruments

The Appalachian **dulcimer** is a folk instrument. It is believed to have originated in the eastern United States. Like the guitar, the dulcimer has strings stretched over the sounding body. Unlike the guitar, the dulcimer does not have a neck. The player plucks the strings with his right hand. He changes the pitch of the strings with his left hand.

Listen for the sound of the dulcimer on your recording of "The Riddle Song."

Bruce Roberts from Rapho Guillumette Pictures, Inc., New York.

Bruce Roberts from Rapho Guillumette Pictures, Inc., New York.

Arnold from Magnum Photos, Inc.

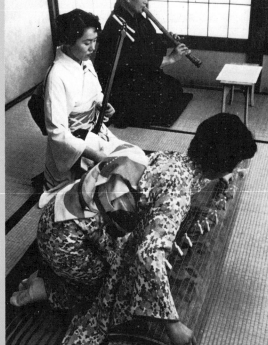

Consulate General of Japan, New York.

The Riddle Song

American Folk Song

1. I gave my love a cher - ry that has no stone; I gave my love a
2. How can there be a cher - ry that has no stone? How can there be a
3. A cher-ry when it's bloom-ing, it has no stone; A chick-en when it's

chick-en that has no bone; I gave my love a ring that
chick-en that has no bone? How can there be a ring that
pip - ping, it has no bone; A ring when it's roll - ing, it

has no end; I gave my love a ba - by with no cry - in'.
has no end? How can there be a ba - by with no cry - in'?
has no end; A ba - by when it's sleep-ing has no cry - in'.

Stringed instruments are played in nearly every part of the world. There is wide variation in the shapes and sounds of these instruments. The **balalaika** of Russia is a tri-angular, guitar-like instrument. The Japanese **koto** is a large, beautiful instrument. It has many strings and is more difficult to play than some other stringed instruments.

 *Tum-Balalaika*   *Sakura*
Under the Apple Tree   *Shin-Takasago*
Russian Folk Songs   *Japanese Folk Songs*

Listen to the sounds of the balalaika and the koto in these compositions. Which of the instruments sound like stringed instruments you know? Describe the sound of each instrument.

The sounds of voices

I the singer stand on high on the yellow rushes;
Let me go forth with noble songs
and laden with flowers.

Aztec Song

Sing! Sing! Sing!

Brazilian Folk Song

Lift up your voice and sing, sing, sing!

Lift up your voice and sing, sing, sing!

1. With rich man and poor man and beg - gar and thief, With
2. With Is - a - bel, An - na - bel, John - ny and Lee, With

doc - tor and law - yer and In - dian chief.
ev - 'ry - one liv - ing, where - e'er they be. } We'll sing, we'll

sing, we'll lift up our voice and sing. sing! We'll

sing! We'll sing! We'll sing! We'll sing!

Using your voice

Songs are a good means of communicating, for they not only have words, but musical expression as well. People find that singing is a means of expressing themselves. "Let Us Sing Together" expresses the joy of being with friends.

Let Us Sing Together

Czech Round

Let us sing to-geth-er, Let us sing to-geth-er, One and all a

joy - ous song. Let us sing to-geth - er, One and all a

joy - ous song. Let us sing a - gain and a - gain,

Let us sing a - gain and a-gain. Let us sing a - gain and a-gain,

One and all a joy - ous song.

Singing is one way people express religious ideas and feelings. People all over the world sing religious songs. Singing is an important part of most religious services.

"Dona Nobis Pacem" was written in the sixteenth century. The Latin words mean "Grant us peace."

Dona Nobis Pacem

Latin Hymn
Attributed to Palestrina

He's Got the Whole World in His Hands

Afro-American Spiritual

1. He's got the whole world in His hands,
2. He's got the wind and rain in His hands,

1. He's got the whole wide world, He's got the whole wide world,
2. He's got the wind and rain, He's got the wind and rain,

He's got the whole world in His hands,
He's got the wind and rain in His hands,

He's got the whole wide world, He's got the whole wide world,
He's got the wind and rain, He's got the wind and rain,

He's got the whole world in His hands,
He's got the wind and rain in His hands,

He's got the whole wide world, He's got the whole wide world,
He's got the wind and rain, He's got the wind and rain,

He's got the whole world in His hands.

He's got the whole world in His hands.

People can tell stories through music. Folk singers change their style of singing according to the song they are performing. Listen to "The Fox," then listen again to "The Riddle Song," page 31. In what way do these singing styles differ?

The Fox

American Folk Song

1. The Fox went out on a chil-ly night, He prayed for the moon for to give him light, For he'd man-y a mile to go that night a-fore he reached the town - o, town - o, town - o, he'd man-y a mile to go that night A-fore he reached the town - o.

2. He ran till he came to a great big bin, Where the ducks and the geese were put there-in. "A cou-ple of you will grease my chin a-fore I leave this town - o, town - o, town - o, •A cou-ple of you will grease my chin A-fore I leave this town - o."

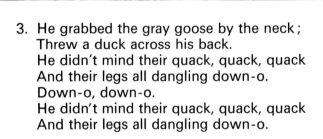

3. He grabbed the gray goose by the neck;
   Threw a duck across his back.
   He didn't mind their quack, quack, quack
   And their legs all dangling down-o.
   Down-o, down-o.
   He didn't mind their quack, quack, quack
   And their legs all dangling down-o.

4. Then old Mother Flipper-Flopper jumped out of bed.
   Out of the window she cocked her head,
   Crying, "John, John! The gray goose is gone
   And the fox is on the town-o!
   Town-o, town-o!"
   Crying, "John, John! The gray goose is gone
   And the fox is on the town-o!"

5. Then John he went to the top of the hill;
   Blew his horn both loud and shrill;
   The fox he said, "I'd better flee with my kill
   Or they'll soon be on my trail-o!
   Trail-o, trail-o!"
   The fox he said, "I'd better flee with my kill
   Or they'll soon be on my trail-o!"

6. He ran till he came to his cozy den,
   There were the little ones, eight, nine, ten.
   They said, "Daddy, better go back again
   'Cause it must be a mighty fine town-o!
   Town-o, town-o!"
   They said, "Daddy, better go back again
   'Cause it must be a mighty fine town-o!"

7. Then the fox and his wife without any strife,
   Cut up the goose with a fork and knife;
   They never had such a supper in their life
   And the little ones chewed on the bones-o.
   Bones-o, bones-o.
   They never had such a supper in their life
   And the little ones chewed on the bones-o.

39

There are many different kinds of singing voices. The range and pitch of a person's voice depend mainly upon the size and shape of his vocal cords.

The voice of a child is **treble**. This means that it has a high range. When boys and girls reach their teens, their voices begin to change, because the vocal chords grow larger and stronger. A noticeable vocal change often takes place with boys. Often, for a few months, some control of the voice is lost. During this time a boy has what is called a "changing voice." Listen to the sound of the changing voice in the second part of "Catch a Falling Star." You can sing this part an octave higher than it is sung on the recording.

Catch a Falling Star

Words and music by
Paul Vance and Lee Pockriss

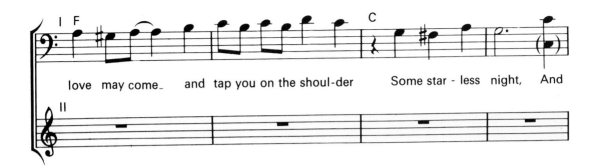

love may come_ and tap you on the shoul-der Some star - less night, And

just in case_ you feel you want to hold her, You'll have a pock-et full of star-light,

You'll have a pock-et full of star-light,

Catch a fall-ing star and put it in your pock-et; Nev-er let it fade a-

Catch a fall-ing star and put it in your pock-et;

Catch a fall-ing star and

Continued on next page

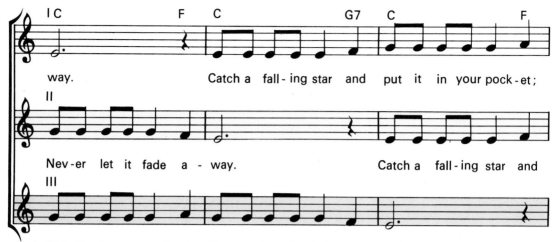

way.

Catch a fall-ing star and put it in your pock-et;

Nev-er let it fade a - way.

Catch a fall-ing star and

Put it in your pock-et; Nev-er let it fade a - way.

Save it for a rain-y day.

put it in your pock-et Save it for a rain-y day, rain-y day.

Catch a fall-ing star and put it in your pock-et; Save it for a rain-y day.

Before a boy's voice changes, he may have a beautiful soprano voice. After his voice changes, he may have a bass or a tenor voice.

Different kinds of songs are suited to different kinds of voices. "Timber" is a work song. What kind of voice would be most suitable for the performance of this song?

Timber

Work Song

1. Got to haul this— tim - ber 'fore the sun— goes down
2. My old mule, he's— strong and al - most nine— feet tall;—

Get it 'cross the riv - er 'fore the boss— comes 'round—
Pulls a lot more tim - ber than a freight— can haul.—

Drag it down that dus - ty— road;
Weighs one thou - sand thir - ty— two—

Come on boys, and let's— haul— this load.—
He's done ev - 'ry - thing a mule— can do.—

Refrain

Tim - ber,— tim - ber,— All that tim - ber's got to roll.

All that tim - ber's got to roll. All that tim - ber's got to roll!

The song "Listen to the Watchman's Cry" can be sung **antiphonally.** This means that one group sings in answer to another group. Create contrasts in dynamics (loudness and softness) so that the answering group will sound like an echo.

Listen to the Watchman's Cry

Words and music by
Isaac Woodbury

Lis-ten! Lis-ten! Lis-ten!

bed." Half past ten! Star-light night!

bed." Half past ten! Star-light night!

Lis-ten to the watch-man's cry.

Lis-ten to the watch-man's cry: "Go to bed, to bed, to bed, to bed."

Lis-ten to the watch-man's cry: "Go to bed, to bed, to bed, to bed."

Continued on next page

Then, kind friends, good night,_____

Good night, good night, good night.

Good night, good night, good night.

Then, kind friends, good night!_____ Good night.

Good night, good night, good night, good night.

Good night, good night, good night, good night.

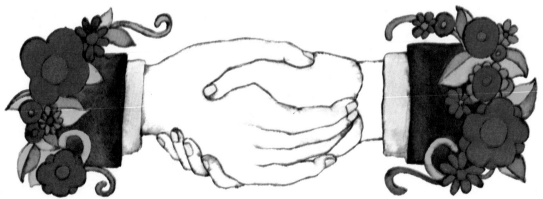

Your singing range

All the notes that you can sing comfortably make up your singing range. When someone sings often, his range becomes wider than that of a person who does not sing very often. This is one reason that some concert singers have very wide ranges. You can check the range of your own voice. Find out how many pitches you can sing comfortably. Begin with middle C and sing down the scale; then begin again with middle C and sing up the scale.

What is your singing range?

Courtesy of Gurtman and Murtha Association, Inc.

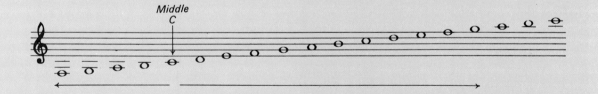

Copy this chart on a piece of music paper. Put a bracket around the notes of your own singing range, and date the paper. Then in a month or two, check your range again. Find out whether it has changed.

Improvising with your voice

EXPERIMENTING WITH VOCAL SOUNDS

You can make interesting sounds with your voice. Find several ways of making voice and mouth sounds. Make pleasing sounds and angry sounds. Create sounds that are frightening and sounds that are sad. Make sounds with your mouth closed, then with your mouth open. After you have experimented with vocal sounds, try the following.

1. Create a mood composition, from one to two minutes long.

2. Choose a setting or a subject for your composition. Your composition might describe a factory, a busy street, the ocean, or Halloween night.

3. Use only sounds that you can make with your voice.

4. Remember to provide unity and variety in your composition. Vary your music by using contrasts in timbre and volume.

Paul Klee Foundation, Museum of Fine Arts, Berne.

Different moods can be expressed by the way the media of art are used and the way the components of art are organized. Some works of art create a mood without containing any recognizable images. This type of art is called <u>non-objective</u>. If the colors in this painting by Paul Klee were changed or the paint brushed on more smoothly, a different mood would be expressed.

Create a non-objective composition. Make geometric shapes on a large piece of manila paper. Use different mixtures of color and experiment with different kinds of brush strokes. Use heavy and light strokes. Work with a brush that is sometimes wet and sometimes almost dry.

MORE VOCAL IMPROVISATION

Here is another way to improvise vocal music. Work with one or two classmates. You may want to tape record your improvisation. Follow these steps.

1. Study the chart below and review the meaning of each symbol.

2. Each person should choose a different square in the chart. Begin at the same time. Make one of the vowel sounds (a, e, i, o, u) as you point to each square and follow the instruction of the symbol.

3. After the improvisation begins, move to another square whenever you wish. When you move to a new square, use another vowel sound and a new pitch.

4. Each person should make at least three moves. The improvisation should last about one minute.

mf	*f*	*p*
$>$	*silence*	$<$
sfz	*mp*	*ff*

mf	mezzo forte	medium loud
f	forte	loud
p	piano	soft
$>$	decrescendo	gradually softer
$<$	crescendo	gradually louder
sfz	sforzando	suddenly loud
mp	mezzo piano	medium soft
ff	fortissimo	very loud

Who?

With great yellow eyes
Staring through the night
The dark owl watches . . . watches . . .
All night he cries
Who? Who?
I wish I knew.

With wild whistling shrieks
Piercing through the night
The cold wind searches . . . searches . . .
All night it howls
Whoooo? Whooooo?
I wish I knew.

Edith Savage

CAREERS

Composers usually have an idea of the kind of music they want to create—a popular song, a symphony, a choral number, an electronic composition. It may be music that accompanies a story, such as an opera, or it may be music composed for its own sake, such as a concerto or a piece for a string quartet. Sometimes music is composed primarily for singing, for dancing, for television, or for advertising. Contemporary composers often write all of these types of music, and for all of these purposes.

Sound Patterns
Pauline Oliveros

Some contemporary composers are experimenting with various ways of using voices. Listen to "Sound Patterns." You will hear many different sounds in this composition. All of these sounds were made by the human voice. This music will give you ideas about new ways of using voices to create compositions.

Experiment with many different kinds of vocal sounds. Then build a composition using some of these sounds. Tape record your composition so that you can listen to it.

Is it interesting? In what ways?

Does it seem to have unity, or hold together?

What gives it unity?

Make changes in your composition if you feel they are needed.

Find a way of writing your composition so that others can perform it.

IMPROVISING MUSIC FOR A POEM

Improvise music for the poem. Here are some ideas.

1. Use a solo-response form, or create echoes.
2. Choose some lines of the poem to repeat at various speeds and dynamic levels.
3. Make up rhythmic or melodic sounds as the background for your composition. Use some unusual vocal sounds in the background.
4. Make up an introduction and a coda.

Another way to use the voice is to explore its range while chanting poetry. Study the poem "Who?" before chanting it. Use the speaking voice almost as you would sing, but do not use definite pitches. Make your voice rise and fall as you say the words of the poem.

Exploring the pipe organ

The **pipe organ** is the oldest of all keyboard instruments. The earliest known ancestor of the organ was developed in Egypt about 2,200 years ago by a young inventor named Ctesibius. While Ctesibius was working in a barber shop, he noticed that the air rushing through a pipe produced a musical tone. This gave him an idea for a new musical instrument. His instrument was called the hydraulis, or water organ, because water pressure was used to force the air through its pipes. The instrument known today as the pipe organ is an instrument capable of producing a wide variety of tonal effects.

The **console** is the part of the organ containing keyboards (called **manuals**), pedal boards (called **pedals**), and **stops**. The manuals are played with the hands; the pedals are played with the feet. The stops, located near the manuals, make it possible for the player to select almost any tone quality desired.

The sound of the pipe organ is produced by blowing air through the pipes. The size and shape of each pipe determine its timbre and pitch.

The pipes are made of metal or wood. Each pipe produces only one tone. Some pipes may be more than 64 feet long; others are shorter than one foot. There may be several thousand pipes for one organ. Pipe organs can be found in churches, concert halls, theaters, restaurants, and private homes.

LISTENING *Toccata in D Minor*
Johann Sebastian Bach

"Toccata in D Minor" is an exciting composition for organ. In this toccata, you will hear some of the sounds that a skillful player can produce on an organ. Johann Sebastian Bach, the great composer who wrote this music, was one of the most famous organists of his day.

During the time of Bach, brass instruments were often used with organs to accompany church singing. "Now Thank We All Our God" is an old hymn which is frequently sung at Thanksgiving services today. Listen to the accompaniment on the recording and identify the instruments you hear.

Now Thank We All Our God

Music *by* Johann Cruger
Words *by* Catherine Winkworth

1. Now thank we all our God, With heart and hands and voic - es,
2. O may this boun-teous God, Through all our life be near us,
3. All praise and thanks to God, The Fa - ther now be giv - en,

Who won-drous things hath done, In whom His world re - joic - es;
With ev - er joy - ful hearts And bless - ed peace to cheer us;
The Son, and Him who reigns With them in high - est heav - en,

Who, from our moth-er's arms, Hath blessed us on our way
And keep us in His grace, And guide us when per - plexed,
The one e - ter - nal God, Whom earth and heaven a - dore;

With count-less gifts of love, And still is ours to - day.
And free us from all ills In this world and the next.
For thus it was, is now, And shall be ev - er - more.

Now Thank We All Our God
Arranged for organ by Johann Sebastian Bach

Now Thank We All Our God
Arranged for theater organ

Composers often borrow melodies for their compositions. Listen to the way Bach used "Now Thank We All Our God" for an organ composition. Compare Bach's version to the modern jazz arrangement.

The organ is an important part of many places of worship. These pictures above show the interiors of two cathedrals in England.

Find the organ pipes in both pictures. Lincoln Cathedral, on the left, was built in the 1100's. Coventry Cathedral was completed in 1962.

Collection, The Museum of Modern Art, New York.

Electronic music

One of the most recent developments in music has been in the field of electronic music. Not long ago, musicians began using electronics to imitate the sounds of ordinary instruments. Today electronic pianos and organs are common.

With the tape recorder, another way of working with sounds became available to composers. Composers tape recorded sounds from the environment such as footsteps, traffic, and sirens. They used these environmental sounds in their compositions. Sometimes these sounds were used alone; sometimes they were combined with other sounds.

EXPERIMENTING WITH A TAPE RECORDER

Here are some ways you can experiment with a tape recorder. Begin by taping a wide variety of sounds. You might tape the sounds of footsteps, bird songs, traffic, sirens, talking, or crying. Use your imagination and collect as many different sounds as possible.

1. Choose a song you know. Make up an accompaniment using classroom instruments. Then select appropriate sounds from your taped collection. They could be part of the accompaniment, or they could be used between the verses of the song. Decide where to insert them. Tape the results on a second tape recorder.

2. Make up an instrumental composition using any of the following.

   A melody instrument (bells, song flute)
   A chordal accompaniment (autoharp, guitar)
   A rhythmic accompaniment (wood block, drum)

   Choose appropriate sounds from your taped collection and include them in this composition. Tape the results.

3. Write some poetry or choose a poem you like. Choose a subject appropriate to your taped sounds. Set the poem to music. You could chant the words as you play an accompaniment, or you could make up a melody and sing the words. Use some of your taped sounds as an accompaniment.

Below are some symbols used to represent electronic sounds. Listen to the recording as each sound is played.

Sine wave　～～～

Sawtooth wave　/W/W/W

Square wave　∏∏∏

White noise　▒▒▒

Electronic music cannot be written in regular music notation. It must be written or diagrammed in a way that shows which sound is to be produced.

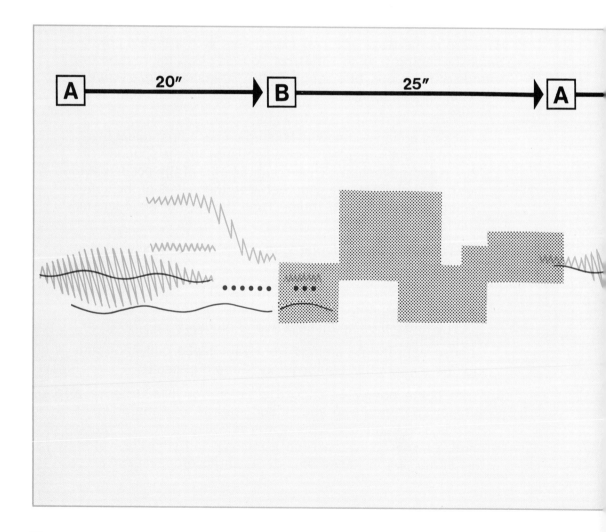

Rondo
David Ernst

As you listen to "Rondo," look at the diagram of the music. Find a design in the diagram which is repeated. In what way is there variation in the repeated design? Describe each section according to the qualities of pitch, duration, volume, and timbre.

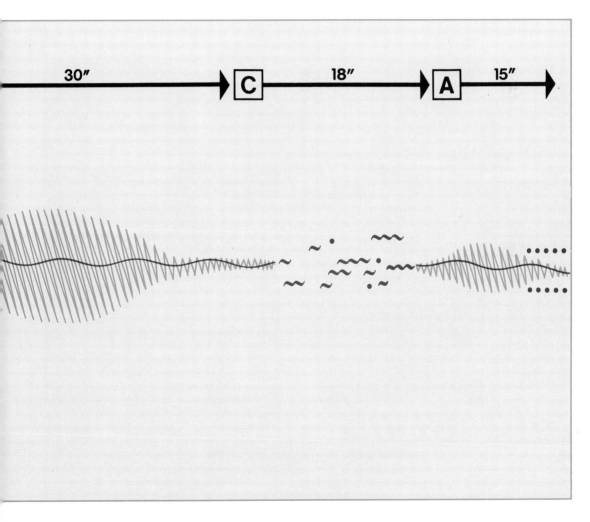

Sonata in E Major
Domenico Scarlatti
Performed on the Moog Synthesizer
by Walter Carlos

Some composers write music in which all the sounds are made electronically. At first composers had to use many different electronic units. Each electronic unit produced a different sound. Then one instrument, the **synthesizer,** was invented. It could produce many different sounds. Listen to this music performed on a synthesizer.

Courtesy of Robert Moog

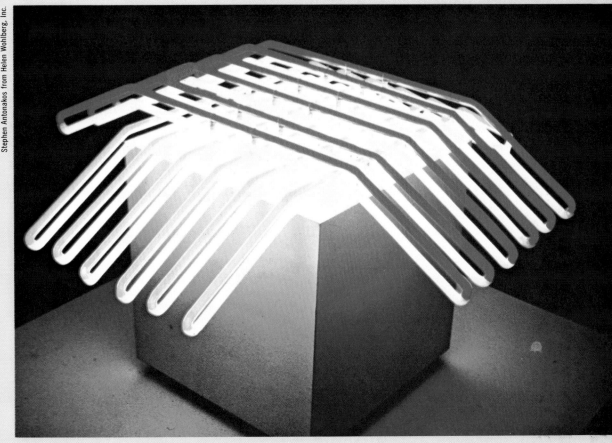

Electricity is often used to move the forms the artist creates. Electricity and lighting can produce striking effects when used by themselves or with reflective materials.

In creating this neon sculpture, the artist filled rods of plexiglass with fluorescent light. The rods are carefully balanced so that when they vibrate, this structure becomes a shimmering form.

This sculpture could only have been created in the past fifty years. Before then the materials did not exist. Create a piece of contemporary art by using materials that did not exist before the 20th century. These could include plastic forks, bubblegum wrappers, flip tops, and band-aids, to name just a few. See how many different products of this century you can find. Then glue them together to make a sculpture or a collage.

The components of music

The components of music are the basic ingredients from which music is made. These ingredients are:

1. Rhythm — The organization of the duration (length) of sounds

2. Melody — a horizontal arrangement of pitches of specific duration

3. Harmony — two or more tones sounded together

4. Expression — tempo, dynamics, articulation

The artist José Clemente Orozco used the components of art to help tell a story. Shapes, colors, lines, and textures all blend together to give the picture a feeling of strength. What do you think this picture is about?

63

Rhythm

All music has rhythm. The rhythm of music consists of sounds and silences of various lengths. One component of rhythm is strong **pulse,** or regular accent.

The strong pulse of music helps people move together. For example, the LEFT-right, LEFT-right feeling of a march is created by a regular accent. As you sing "Marching to Pretoria," listen for the regular accents.

Marching to Pretoria

South African Folk Tune
Words by Joseph Marais

1. I'm with you and you're with me, And so we are all to - geth - er,
2. We have food, the food is good, And so we will eat to - geth - er,

So we are all to - geth - er, So we are all to - geth - er;
So we will eat to - geth - er, So we will eat to - geth - er;

Sing with me, I'll sing with you And so we will sing to - geth - er,
When we eat, 'twill be a treat And so let us sing to - geth - er,

Refrain

As we march a - long. _____ We are march-ing to Pre -
As we march a - long. _____

to - ri - a, _____ Pre - to - ri - a, _____ Pre - to - ri - a, _____ We are

march-ing to Pre - to - ri - a, _____ Pre - to - ri - a, Hur - rah! _____

Meter in music

Strong pulse in music divides beats into groups of 2's and 3's, and combinations of such groups. This grouping of beats is called **meter.** In written music, a bar line is placed before normally strong beats. Bar lines group beats into measures. A **meter signature** shows what the grouping in each measure will be.

$\frac{2}{4}$ = 2 quarter notes or their equal in each measure

$\frac{4}{4}$ = 4 quarter notes or their equal in each measure

$\frac{3}{4}$ = 3 quarter notes or their equal in each measure

$\frac{2}{2}$ = 2 half notes or their equal in each measure

What symbols are missing from the song below? How can you decide where they should be placed?

After you have learned "Music Alone Shall Live," sing it as a two-part round.

Music Alone Shall Live
(Himmel und Erde)

German Canon

1. All things shall per - ish from un - der the sky;
Him - mel und Er - de müs - sen ver - gehn;

2. Mu - sic a - lone shall live, Mu - sic a - lone shall live,
a - ber die Mus - i - ci, a - ber die Mus - i - ci,

Mu - sic a - lone shall live, nev - er to die.
a - ber die Mus - i - ci, blei - ben be - stehn.

Artists create rhythm in a work by repeating shapes, lines, colors, or textures. An architect often repeats visual units in a building. The Boston Public Library and the Dulles International Airport are examples of the repetition of visual units. Where do you see repetition in these buildings? Look around your community for buildings that contain repeated units in their designs. If possible, take some pictures of these buildings and discuss them in class.

Changing meter

Look at the different meter signatures in "Shenandoah."
How many times does the meter change?

This song describes a person's longing to return to his
home in the valley.

Shenandoah

American Sea Chantey

1. Oh, Shen-an-doah, I long to see you,— And— hear your roll-ing
2. Oh, Shen-an-doah, I miss your val-ley,— A - way, you roll-ing
3. Oh, Shen-an-doah, I love your daugh-ter,— A - way, you roll-ing

riv-er,____ Oh, Shen-an-doah, I long to see you, — A-
riv-er,____ Oh, Shen-an-doah, I miss your val-ley, — A-
riv-er,____ Oh, Shen-an-doah, I love your daugh-ter____ A-

way, we're bound a-way, 'Cross the wide Mis-sou-ri.____
way, we're bound a-way, 'Cross the wide Mis-sou-ri.____
way, we're bound a-way, 'Cross the wide Mis-sou-ri.____

4. For seven long years I've been a-roving,
   Away, you rolling river,
   For seven long years I've been a-roving,
   Away, we're bound away, 'Cross the wide Missouri.

A changing meter can make a melody seem to have more freedom. How would a conductor conduct this song? Conduct the music as you listen to the recording. Use these conducting patterns.

Remember that your hand should go down on the first beat of each measure.

Fiesta Time

Mexican Folk Melody
Words by Laura Johnson

Lan - terns___ are shin-ing bright-ly, Breez - es____ are blow-ing

light - ly, Mu - sic___ is play-ing night - ly,___ Be - cause it's

now Fi - es - ta Time in old San Juan.___ Come to the

pla - za___ with-out de-lay - ing,___ Here in the pla - za___ gui - tars are

Photo Fred Fehl

play - ing. Lis - ten____ to what they're say - ing____ Be - cause it's

now fi - es - ta time in old San Juan.

This Mexican folk song can be accompanied with auto-harp and maracas. The autoharp can be strummed with the metric beat.

AUTOHARP

MARACAS

Irregular meter

Most of the music you hear has a regular meter throughout the whole piece.

$$\frac{4}{4} \qquad \frac{2}{2} \qquad \frac{3}{4}$$

But sometimes music has an **irregular meter**. Irregular meter adds interest to music. Listen to "The Shepherd Boy." Decide which beats are accented in each measure.

The Shepherd Boy

Greek Folk Song
Translated by
Aristides E. Phoutrides
Words Adapted

1. Once I was a shep-herd boy,_____ I kept my sheep but_____
2. Now I spend my days in sing - ing, I play my flute till the

knew no joy;___ Then one day a ___ maid - en found_ me,___
hills are ring-ing, For one day a ___ maid - en found_ me,___

Charmed me, and __ her bright eyes bound me.__
Charmed me, and __ her bright eyes bound me.__ }*Tun - de, tun - de,

tun - de, tun - de!__ Tun - de, tun - de tun - de tun - de!

* (Toon-day).

Waltz
William Russell

The Blue Danube
Johann Strauss

One of the most familiar meters in music is $\frac{3}{4}$, or triple meter. This means that there are three metric beats in each measure. This meter is often referred to as "waltz time," because the waltz step is danced in triple meter.

The two waltzes that are recorded here are quite different from each other. Listen to the two compositions to discover the answers to the questions.

1. Which is the traditional waltz in $\frac{3}{4}$ meter?
2. How is the meter of the other composition different?
3. What instruments can you identify in each of these compositions?

Martha Swope

Melodic rhythm

Every melody has its own rhythm which is called the **melodic rhythm.** Sing "Hold Tight." Clap the melodic rhythm. How are the phrases alike?

Hold Tight
(Tenès la de près)

French Folk Song

Hold tight to your girl when you have her,
Te - nès la de près, vaous - tra mi - o,

Hold tight to the girl that you have, _____
Te - nès la de près quand l'au - rès. _____

It may be possible to recognize a song by hearing or seeing its melodic rhythm. Is this the rhythm of "Polly Wolly Doodle" or "Yankee Doodle"?

What song has this melodic rhythm?

Clap the melodic rhythm of a familiar song and ask someone to identify it.

"The Green Violinist" was painted by Marc Chagall, who was born in Russia. As a child, Chagall lived in a village like the one in the background of this painting.

Why does this look like a painting of a magic fiddler? What are your feelings when you see unexpected objects such as a man with a green face, and houses and people floating in air? This is a fantasy picture. Paint your own fantasy picture. Experiment with colored inks or transparent watercolors.

1. Use a pencil and draw lightly the objects you wish to include in your painting.

2. Use light watercolor or ink to paint your whole paper.

3. After this background has dried, paint objects over it. Use various colors of transparent paint or ink.

Syncopated rhythm

Some music has a syncopated rhythm. This means that accents in the music fall on notes that are not normally accented. **Syncopation** helps to make music more exciting.

Look at the rhythmic notation below. Each pair of lines contains one example of syncopation. Clap the lines or play them on a drum. Which pattern of each pair is syncopated?

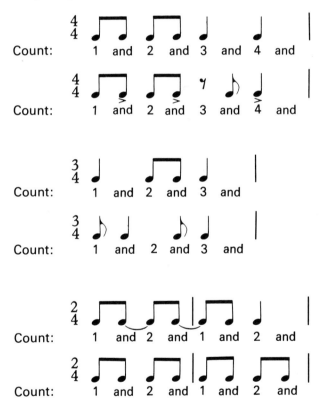

Syncopation is usually not identified by accent marks, as in the first example above. The music is arranged so that the accents will fall in unusual places.

The syncopation in "Rock-a-My Soul" is written in these two ways.

Ties, short-long note patterns, and rests are ways of creating syncopation. Look for them in other songs.

If you clap on beats ONE and THREE as you sing "Rock-a-My Soul," the syncopation will seem even stronger.

Rock-a-My Soul

Afro-American Spiritual

Rock-a-my soul_ in the bo-som of A - bra-ham; Rock-a-my soul_ in the

bo-som of A - bra-ham; Rock-a-my soul_ in the bo-som of A - bra-ham;

Oh, rock-a my soul _____ So high,

Melody

Oh, rock-a my soul.
1. My Lord is so high, you can't get o - ver Him;
2. His love is so high, you can't get o - ver it.

So low, So wide,

So low, you can't get un - der Him; So wide, you
So low, you can't get un - der it; So wide, you

You must go in at the door.

can't get a - round_ Him; You must go in at the door.
can't get a - round_ it; You must go in at the door.

Folk music from many countries contains syncopated rhythms. This song is very energetic and calls for a spirited dance. The words mean "Rise, my friends. Let us dance around and around, and work another day."

Kuma Echa

Words by Y. Scheinberg
Arranged by S. L. Postolsky

Ku - ma e - cha sov__ va - sov Al__ ta - nu - cha sho - va shov.

Eyn__ kan roch v'- eyn__ kan sof Yad__ el yad__ al ta - a'- zov,

Yom__ sha - ka v'- yom__ yiz - rach A - nu ne - fen ach__ el ach

Min__ ha - k'far u - min__ ha - k'rach B'- cher - mesh u - va - a'- nach.

How many times do you find the syncopated eighth-quarter-eighth note pattern ♪ ♩ ♪ or a variation of it ♫ ♩ ♪ in "Kuma Echa"?

This sculpture has a feeling of rhythm. The viewer's eyes move from one rounded shape to another. The shapes are grouped so that the viewer's eyes also move from group to group.

The base on which the sculpture stands is quite different in feeling from the piece itself. Describe the base. What effect does the base have on the feeling of the sculpture?

81

Calypso music began in the West Indies. True calypso songs are improvised. They often tell about things that are happening. The first calypso singers were, in a way, "singing newsboys," for they sang about current events. Calypso music contains a great deal of syncopation.

Use rhythm patterns from the song to make up a calypso-type accompaniment. Here are some examples. Which of these have syncopation?

Some measures in "Island in the Sun" do not contain syncopation. These unsyncopated measures make the syncopated measures seem stronger by contrast. Which measures do not contain syncopation?

Island in the Sun

Music by Harry Belafonte
Words by Lord Burgess

1. This is my is - land in the sun where my peo-ple have toiled since

time be - gun.__ Though I may sail on man-y a sea __ Her

shores will al - ways be home to me.__

Oh, is - land in the sun, __ Willed to me __ by my

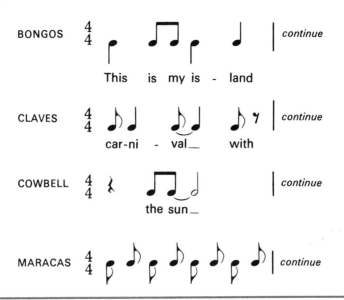

BONGOS   4/4   continue

This is my is - land

CLAVES   4/4   continue

car-ni - val__ with

COWBELL   4/4   continue

the sun__

MARACAS   4/4   continue

D   G
fa - ther's hand._   All my days_ I will sing in praise of your

A7   D   Fine
for - ests, wat - ers, your shin - ing sand._

D   G   A7
2. I hope the day will nev - er come that I can't a - wake to the

D   A7
sound of drum. Nev - er let__ me miss car - ni - val__ With ca -

D   A7   D   D.S. al Fine
lyp - so songs__ phil - o - soph - i - cal.__

Triplets

Look at the notes in "Carmen, Carmela." Find the groups of notes that look like this.

The small 3 above a group of notes tells that the three notes are played in the same amount of time that two of the same notes normally receive. These groups of three notes are called **triplets**.

Listen for the triplets in the recording of "Carmen, Carmela."

Carmen, Carmela

Mexican Folk Song
English text by Alfred Clure

When all the bright gold-en sun-beams fade in the west, and
A - sí cual mue - ren en oc - ci - den - te los ti - bios

day slow-ly turns to night, I still re - mem - ber your face, your
ra - yos del as - tro rey. A - sí mu - rie - ron mis i - lu -

soft, charm-ing grace, a mem - 'ry of fond de - light,
sio - nes, a - sí ex-tin - guién - do - se va mi fé.

84

Refrain

C7 ... F

Car - men, Car - mel - a _____ please hear my yearn - ing, ___
Car - men, Car - mel - a, _____ Luz de mis o - jos, ___

C7 ... F

___ your rad - iant beau - ty _____ has blind - ed me.
___ si luz no hu - bie - ra, _____ Ha - bías de ser.

C7 ... F

Car - men, Car - mel - a, _____ my love I give you; ___
Her - mo - so fa - ro _____ De ven - tu - ran - za, ___

C7 ... F

___ please give me your love _____ and set me free. _____
___ Dul - ce es - pe - ran - za, _____ Be - llo pla - cer. _____

Mussels are small shellfish. The people who live on the coast of France collect mussels to eat or to sell.

Find the triplets in this song.

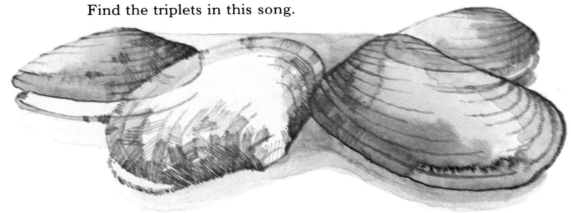

I've Been To Gather Mussels
(A la Pêche des Moules)

French Folk Song

Refrain

I've been to ga - ther mus - sels,   Don't want to go a - gain Ma - ma,
A   la   pê - che   des   mou - les,   Je   ne veux plus al - ler   Ma - man,

I've been to ga - ther mus - sels,   Don't want to go a - gain.
A   la   pê - che   des   mou - les,   Je   ne veux plus al - ler.

Verse

Those bad boys from the vil - lage,   Steal-ing my bag for fun, Ma - ma,
Les   gar - çons de Ma - ren - nes,   M'ont pris___ mon pa - nier, Ma - man,

Those bad boys from the vil - lage,   Steal-ing my bag for fun!
Les   gar - çons de Ma - ren - nes,   M'ont pris___ mon pa - nier!

2. They kiss you and they whisper
   You are the girl for them, Mama,
   They kiss you and they whisper
   You are the girl for them.

3. They hug you, oh, so tightly,
   How can I trust them then, Mama?
   They hug you, oh, so tightly,
   How can I trust them then?

4. For boys are as the wind blows,
   Fickle as April rain, Mama,
   For boys are as the wind blows,
   Fickle as April rain.

5. But girls are true forever
   Faithful and true remain, Mama.
   But girls are true forever
   Faithful and true remain.

2. *Ils vous font des caresses,*
   Des petits compliments, Maman,
   Ils vous font des caresses,
   Des petits compliments.

3. *Quand un' fois ils vous tiennent,*
   Sont-ils de bons enfants, Maman?
   Quand un' fois ils vous tiennent,
   Sont-ils de bons enfants?

4. *Les garçons sont volages*
   Comm' la poudre au vent, Maman.
   Les garçons sont volages
   Comm' la poudre au vent.

5. *Mais les fill' sont fideles*
   Comm' l'or et l'argent, Maman.
   Mais les fill' sont fideles
   Comm' l'or et l'argent.

"Once to Every Man and Nation" presents a stirring challenge to seek truth and defend it with courage. The words were written by James Russell Lowell, a famous American writer of the nineteenth century. Even though these words were written in 1845, they seem challenging today.

Once to Every Man and Nation

Welsh Hymn Melody
Words by James Russell Lowell

1. Once to _____ ev - ery man and _____ na - tion
2. Then to _____ side with truth is _____ no - ble,
3. Though the _____ cause of e - vil _____ pros - per,

Comes the _____ mo - ment to _____ de - cide,
When we _____ share ___ her wretch - ed crust,
Yet 'tis _____ truth ___ a - lone ___ is strong;

In the _____ strife of truth with _____ false - hood,
Ere her _____ cause bring fame and _____ prof - it,
Though her _____ por - tion be the _____ scaf - fold,

For the _____ good ___ or e - vil side;
And 'tis _____ pros - p'rous to ___ be just;
And up - on ___ the throne ___ be wrong.

The meter signature of this song indicates that there are four half notes in each measure.

$$\frac{4}{2} \quad \textbf{\textonehalf} \quad \textbf{\textonehalf} \quad \textbf{\textonehalf} \quad \textbf{\textonehalf} \ |$$

In this song there are triplets of quarter notes.

$$\overbrace{\ \textbf{♩}\ \textbf{♩}\ \textbf{♩}\ }^{3} = \textbf{\textonehalf}$$

Music without meter

"O Come, O Come, Emmanuel" is an example of early church music. This was the most important type of music during the early Middle Ages (600 – 1000 A.D.).

Here is a picture of part of a music manuscript dating from 1100 A.D. At that time, written music contained little indication of rhythm. It is thought that the melodies took their rhythm from the rhythm of the words. In this kind of music, there is no metric beat.

In the music below, stems have been omitted from the notes to indicate freedom from meter. This mark ' tells the singers to pause.

O Come, O Come, Emmanuel

Ancient Plainchant

O come, O come, Em man - u - el, and ran - som cap - tive
Ve - ni, Ve - ni, Em - man - u - el, Cap - ti - vum sol - ve

Is - ra - el, That mourns in lone - ly ex - ile here
Is - ra - el, Qui ge - mit in ex - i - li - o,

Un - til the Son of God_____ ap - pear. Re - joice! Re - joice!
Pri - va - tus De - i Fi - li - o. Gau - de! Gau - de!

Em - man - u - el Shall come to thee, O Is - ra - el.
Em - man - u - el Nas - ce - tur pro te, Is - ra - el.

Melody

A melody is a succession of pitches that move in time. Each tone in a melody has both pitch and duration.

Most melodies are built from pitch arrangements called **scales.** There are many kinds of scales. You are familiar with major scales and minor scales. Listen to the melody of "Tum-Balalaika" to find out whether it is based upon a major scale or a minor scale.

Tum-Balalaika

Jewish Folk Song

Boys: Maid - en, maid - en, can you ex - plain,
Girls: Fool - ish boy, I can___ ex - plain, A

What can grow with-out an - y rain? What ___ can burn for man-y a year?
stone can grow with-out an - y rain. True love can burn for man-y a year. A

The melody of the song "Tum-Balalaika" is based on this minor scale.

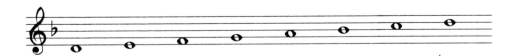

Modes

"Scarborough Fair" is an old English song. There are many different versions of the words and the melody.

"Scarborough Fair" is based on this scale.

Play this scale. How is it different from the minor scale on page 93? The scale above is called the dorian **mode**. There are many kinds of modes. Each mode uses a different pattern of intervals.

Scarborough Fair

English Folk Song

1. Are you go - ing to Scar - bor -ough Fair?_____ Pars - ley,
2. Tell her to make me a cam - bric shirt. _____ Pars - ley,

sage, rose-mar - y and thyme;___ Re - mem - ber me to one that lives
sage, rose-mar - y and thyme;___ With - out a seam or fine nee - dle

there,_____ For she was once a true love of mine._____
work,_____ And then she'll be a true love of mine._____

94

3. Tell her to wash it in yonder dry well,
   Parsley, sage, rosemary and thyme;
   Where water ne'er sprung, nor drop of rain fell,
   And then she'll be a true love of mine.

4. Tell her to dry it on yonder thorn,
   Parsley, sage, rosemary and thyme;
   Which never bore blossom since Adam was born,
   And then she'll be a true love of mine.

5. Tell him to find me an acre of land,
   Parsley, sage, rosemary and thyme;
   Between the sea foam and the sea sand,
   Or never be a true love of mine.

6. Tell him to plough it with a lam'b horn,
   Parsley, sage, rosemary and thyme;
   And sow it all over with one peppercorn,
   Or never be a true love of mine.

7. Tell him to reap it with a sickle of leather,
   Parsley, sage, rosemary and thyme;
   And tie it all up with a peacock's feather,
   Or never be a true love of mine.

8. When he has done and finished his work,
   Parsley, sage, rosemary and thyme;
   Then come to me for his cambric shirt,
   And he shall be a true love of mine.

"The Ol' Gray Goose" is an American folk song.
Write some verses of your own for this nonsense song.

The Ol' Gray Goose

American Folk Song

1. Asked Miss Sus - an one fine day To join me for a ride;
2. She was clim - bin' from the cart, Miss Sus - an lost her shoe;

Found she was so ver - y fat I could-n't sit in - side.
Stock - in' had a big round hole, Her foot was stick-in' through.

Refrain

Oh, look-a here, Oh, look-a there, Look way o - ver yon - der;

Don't you see the ol' gray goose A - smil - ing at the gan - der?

"The Ol' Gray Goose" is also built on a mode. It is
called the mixolydian mode. Find it on page 97 and
look at its pattern of intervals.

Reviewing scales

You have played, sung, and heard music based on many different scales.

Play the scales below. Listen to their sounds.

Major scale

Minor scale

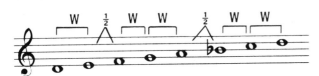

Dorian mode

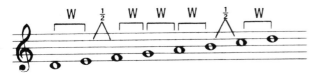

Mixolydian mode

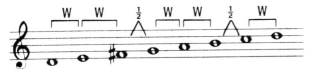

A scale may start on any tone. Play some of these scales, starting on different tones.

Choose one of the scales and improvise a melody.

Pentatonic scales

Not all scales have seven tones. The melody of the Chinese folk song "The Flower Gift" is built on a five-tone scale. Five-tone scales are called **pentatonic scales.** Much music from the Far East uses pentatonic scales.

The Flower Gift

Chinese Folk Song
English words adapted

Sweet scent-ed flowers I___ bring to you, To - ken are

they of our friend - ship true; Fra - grant in the___

morn - ing___ air, Pet - als del - i - cate with beau - ty rare.

Flow-ers I bring in___ friend - ship true, Love - ly___

flowers I___ give to you.

This is the pentatonic scale on which "The Flower Gift" is based.

Here are four ostinatos. Any of these can be used to accompany this song.

Resonator Bells
or Metallophone

Melody Bells
or Glockenspiel

Xylophone
or Temple Blocks

Plucked Strings

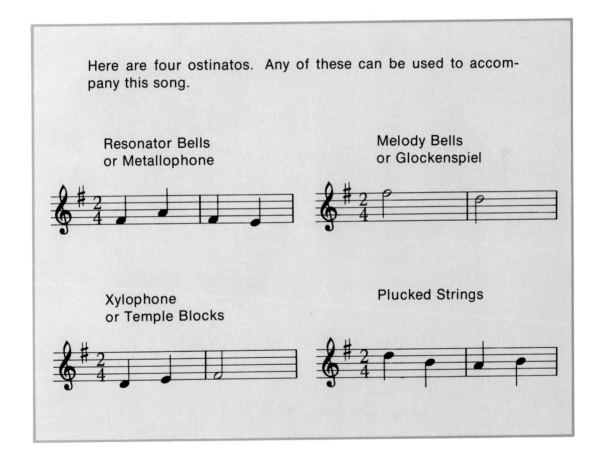

Experiment with different ways of using these ostinatos. Play one or more of them as an introduction before you start to sing. Compose an ending, or a coda, following the song. Try various combinations of instruments. Make up other ostinatos using the pentatonic scale shown at the top of the page.

The city of Cuzco, located high in the mountains of Peru, is inhabited primarily by Indians. Many years ago, an annual summer festival was held in the public square of the city. People traveled great distances to join the celebration. A large conch shell was blown to announce the event. This song was sung during the festivities.

Blow on the Sea Shell

Words by Christine Turner Curtis
Inca Folk Melody

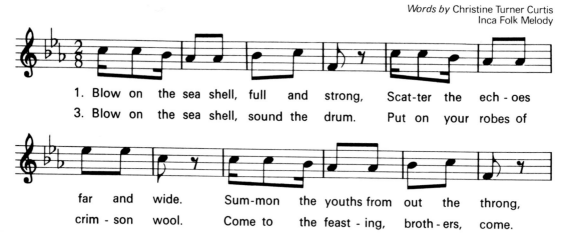

1. Blow on the sea shell, full and strong, Scat-ter the ech - oes
3. Blow on the sea shell, sound the drum. Put on your robes of

far and wide. Sum-mon the youths from out the throng,
crim - son wool. Come to the feast - ing, broth - ers, come.

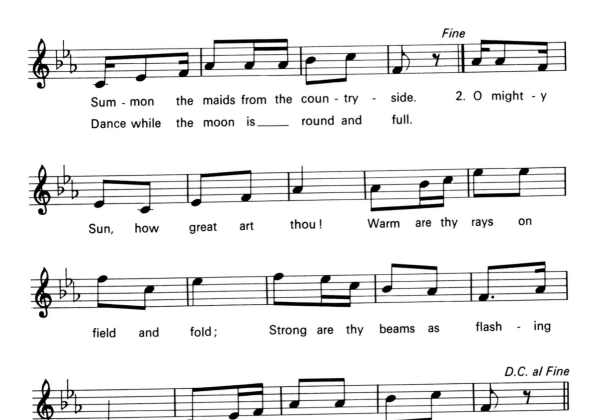

Sum - mon   the maids from the coun - try - side.   2. O might - y
Dance while   the moon is____ round and   full.

Sun,   how   great   art   thou !   Warm   are thy   rays   on

field   and   fold;   Strong   are thy   beams   as   flash - ing

D.C. al Fine

spears,   Bright   is thy   face   as   bur - nished   gold.

Music based on scales is built around a **tonal center**. The first tone of the scale is its tonal center.

Look on page 98 to find the tonal center of the song "The Flower Gift."

This is the scale for "Blow on the Sea Shell."

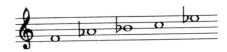

What is the tonal center of "Blow on the Sea Shell"?

COMPOSING WITH PENTATONIC SCALES

You may work with three or four other pupils to compose a pentatonic composition. Begin by building a pentatonic scale. Write your scale on music paper.

1. Make up several simple ostinatos that contain two or three of the pitches in your pentatonic scale. Each ostinato should have a different rhythm pattern. Here are some suggestions for ostinatos.

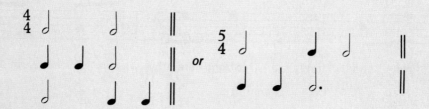

2. Make up a short melody based on your pentatonic scale. Create two or three ostinatos to accompany it. Organize a composition using your ostinatos, your melody, and one or two percussion instruments, such as finger cymbals and rattles.

The form of your work could be as follows:

Introduction (ostinatos)

Melody (improvised) with ostinato accompaniment

Coda (ostinatos)

Evaluate your composition. Make improvements. Play your composition for the rest of the class.

Yorishige Saito

The predominant visual feature of the Japanese temple is its roof. Each floor of the temple has a roof extension. Although the lines of this building are primarily vertical, the horizontal roof lines provide a countermovement. This vertical and horizontal contrast helps give the buildings their unique character. All the buildings in this picture look balanced and unified.

"Sakura" is a famous Japanese folk song. This song is a delicate musical picture of cherry blossom time in Japan. What are the tones of the pentatonic scale used in "Sakura"?

Sakura

Japanese Folk Song

Sa - ku - ra,   Sa - ku - ra,   Now is cher - ry blos-som__ time,
Sa - ku - ra,   Sa - ku - ra,   Ya - yo - i - no   so - ra___ wa,

Clouds of pet - als fill the__ sky;   Per - fume floats like   mist in__ air,
Mi - wa - ta - su ka - gi - ri;   Ka - su - mi - ka   ku - mo__ ka,

Blos - soms fra - grant ev - 'ry - where;   Sa - ku - ra,   Sa - ku - ra,
Ni - o - i - zo   i - zu - ru;   I - za - ya,   I - za - ya,

Beau - ty   in   the   spring   -   time.
Mi -   - ni   -   -   yu   -   -   kan.

A simple two-tone accompaniment for "Sakura" can be played by plucking the A and E strings of a violin, an autoharp, or another stringed instrument. Finger cymbals might be played on the third beat of each measure to add a delicate sound.

The Japanese painting, "Woman with Scroll" by Toyonobu, has a unique character. It is quite rhythmic. It utilizes light, soft colors and flowing lines. The artist used ink or color washes and worked exclusively with a soft hair brush.

Paint a picture using only brush lines and light watercolors. Paint the same subject using a hard marking instrument—a ball point pen, a hard lead pencil, a stiff pen, or a hard crayon. How is the character of each work different?

Tone row

Some music has no tonal center. This music is built on
a **tone row.**

BUILDING A TONE ROW

You can make up a tone row in this way.

1. Pick out the black and white resonator bells within the octave from middle C♯ to the C above; scramble them.

2. Give one bell and a mallet to each of twelve people; have them stand in a row without looking at the names of the resonator bells.

3. Starting at one end of the line, let each person play his or her bell once. The pitches played are a tone row.

4. Play your row forward and backward.

5. Use your row to play the melodic rhythm of a familiar song, such as "Are You Sleeping?" Play just one note on each bell. When all the tones in the row have been used, start at the beginning of the line again.

6. Use your row to play the melodic rhythm of familiar songs.

The tone row was first developed by an Austrian composer, Arnold Schoenberg. Now many composers use tone rows as a basis for their music.

LISTENING ***Canon: The Parting of the Ways***
Arnold Schoenberg

This short vocal piece was written by Arnold Schoenberg. "Canon" is a musical joke. It was intended to make fun of composers who tried to write twelve-tone music with no key feeling, but who could not get away from key feeling.

Here is the tone row Schoenberg used in "Canon." The first three notes should tell you this is a joke. Why?

How many voices sing this "Canon"?

In Mondrian's "Composition in a Square," rectangles are arranged so that they relate to each other. Only a few colors are used. There is no part which is more important than any other. Because this type of painting has no recognizable subject matter, the artist called it simply "composition."

Make a visual composition of your own. Place long strips of black paper horizontally and vertically on a sheet of white paper so that the surface is divided into rectangles or squares. Move the strips around until you have a pleasing organization of black and white. Cut a few shapes from red, yellow, or blue paper and place them on your composition. Paste your composition together.

Spider's web of silk
Lustrous pearls you wear each morn
Could you but keep them.

Don Rosine

"The Web" is based upon a tone row. Read the words
of the song. Why was a tone row a good choice for setting
this poem to music?

The Web

(excerpt)

Music by David Ward-Steinman
Words by Susan Lucas

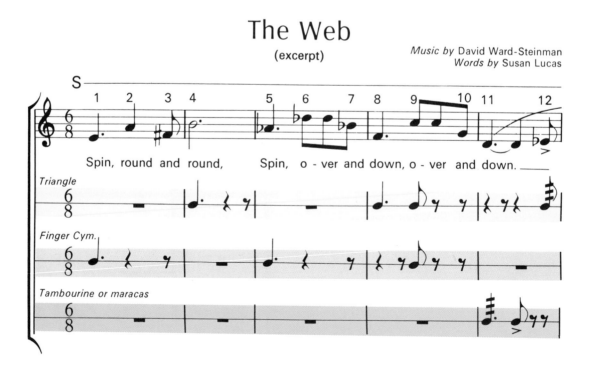

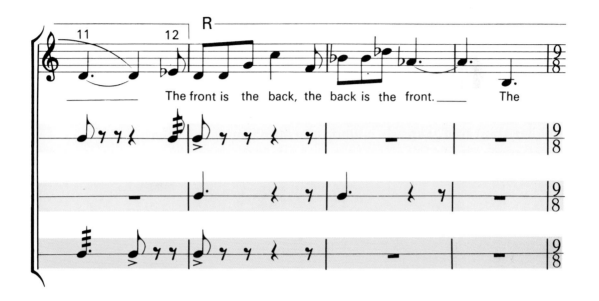

The front is the back, the back is the front.____ The

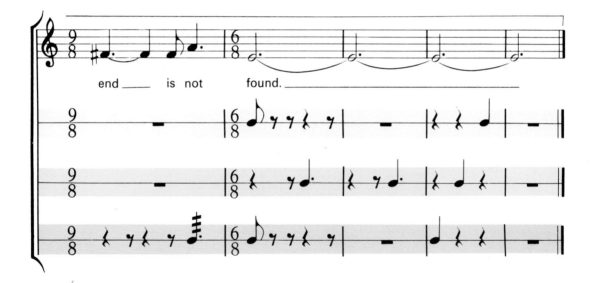

end ____ is not found. ____

LISTENING *The Web*
David Ward-Steinman

This is a two-part arrangement of "The Web." As you
listen to the recording, think about how effectively the
composer has used words. Why do you think the last word of
the second voice part is whispered and not sung?

Microtonal music

Some composers make up their own scales. The American composer Harry Partch used a scale which has forty-three pitches to each octave. His music, based on intervals smaller than half steps, is called **microtonal music**. Microtonal music sounds out of tune to people who listen only to music built from half and whole steps.

LISTENING *Study on an Ancient Greek Scale*
Harry Partch

"Study on an Ancient Greek Scale" is a microtonal composition. The piece is played on instruments that the composer invented.

Courtesy of Danlee Mitchell

Could you play this music on a piano? Why do you think Harry Partch built his own instruments?

Anthony J. Paccione

Harmony

Harmony is heard when two or more pitches are sounded together.   Harmony is an important way of adding interest to music.

Harmony with rounds and descants

"Sing Together" is a song you may know. Sing it in unison, as it is written on this page.

This song can also be sung as a round. A round is one way to make harmony. Page 113 shows the song written as a three-part round. Follow your part as you sing the round.

Sing Together

Traditional Round

Sing, sing to - geth - er; mer - ri - ly, mer - ri - ly sing;

Sing, sing to - geth - er; mer - ri - ly, mer - ri - ly sing.

Sing, Sing, Sing, Sing.

Henry Moore used two different visual ideas in "The Bride." The major portion of the sculpture is made up of solid, rounded forms. The other part consists of thin, straight wires. The wires give a feeling of lightness that contrasts with the heavier basic form.

Make a piece of sculpture using two different kinds of materials. Use clay, soap, or wood for a solid basic shape. Contrast this basic shape with a light material such as thin wire, fish line, string, wood strips, thin strips of plastic, or aluminum foil.

"The Peddler" is an English round made up of street cries. Listen for the many different rhythm patterns that occur together as you sing this round.

The Peddler

English Round
Words by H. Lane Wilson

Buy!____ buy, buy, buy! See what you want be - fore you buy.

Ground i - vy, ground i - vy, a cure for the tooth-ache, Or a

drop for your eye; A ring for your sweet-heart, A brooch for your wife;_

Pegs and ket-tles, the fin-est in town; A ker-chief, and a kir - tle, and a

rib-bon and a lace, For half____ a crown! For half____ a crown!

© Erich Hartmann/MAGNUM PHOTOS, INC.

CAREERS

A **choral director** chooses selections, and rehearses and conducts a chorus and the accompanying musicians in performances. Choral directors often give voice lessons and work in music schools and with religious groups.

The Cries of London (excerpt)
Richard Dering

Richard Dering was an English composer in the time of Queen Elizabeth I. He used a variety of street cries to create his clever composition. The piece is performed by five voices and five stringed instruments on the recording. Listen to the way the instruments and the voices are used. As you listen, imagine you are walking down a crowded London street many years ago.

Here are some of the words you will hear.

What do you lack do you buy, sir; see what you lack.
Pins, points, garters, Spanish gloves or silk ribbons..

Will you buy any fine silk stocks, sir?

New oysters, new. Lily-white mussels, new.

Have you any work for a tinker?

What kitchen stuff have you, maids?

Will you buy a mat for a bed?
Brooms! Old boots, old shoes.

Hot pippin-pies, hot. Hot pudding-pies, hot.

Use the dictionary to find the meanings of the old English words you don't know.

Here is a rhythm round. Clap it first in unison. Then clap it as a round.

You may perform this as a four-part round using percussion instruments or other sounds. Try the suggestions below. Then develop your own ideas.

Percussion

1. Wood blocks and castanets
2. Triangles and finger cymbals
3. Maracas and other rattles
4. Tambourines

Body-sounds

1. Click tongues
2. "Shhh" with voices
3. Clap softly
4. Rub palms together

"Golden Slumbers" originated in England during the seventeenth century, and was brought to America by the early settlers. The song is arranged here with a descant, or a **countermelody.** This is another way of making harmony. In this music each melody has its own rhythmic structure.

Golden Slumbers

Quietly

English Folk Song

Descant

Gol - den slum - bers kiss___ your eyes,   Smiles a -

Melody

Gol - den slum - bers kiss   your eyes,   Smiles a - wait   you

wait when you rise.   Sleep, pret- ty dar - ling, do   not cry,   And

when   you rise.   Sleep, pret-ty   dar - ling, do___ not cry,___ And

I   will sing   you lul - la - by.   Lul - la - by,

I   will   sing you   lul - la - by.   Lul - la - by,

Lul - la - by,   Lul -   la - by.

Lul - la -   by,   Lul -   la - by.

Harmony with chords

Melodies may be harmonized with **chords.** Chords are combinations of pitches. You have sung "Sing Together" as a round. Here is the melody of the same song with chordal harmony.

Sing, sing to - geth - er; mer - ri - ly, mer - ri - ly sing;

Sing, sing to - geth - er; mer - ri - ly, mer - ri - ly sing.

Sing, Sing, Sing, Sing.

The chords below consist of three tones each. The distance from one tone to another is called an **interval.** Each tone of the chords below is an interval of a third from its neighbor. Such chords are called **triads.** Find these triads in the song above.

G chord   D chord

The name of each chord is taken from the letter name of the scale tone on which it is built. This tone is called the **chord root.** Build some trials using notes other than G and D as chord roots.

120

Sing "Worried Man Blues." Then divide into two groups. While one group sings the melody, the other group can sing the words of the song on the pitches of the chord roots (autoharp markings printed above the music). The chords and roots on which these are based are:

Worried Man Blues

American Folk Song

It takes a wor-ried man __ to sing a wor-ried song; __ It takes a wor-ried man __ to sing a wor-ried song; __ It takes a wor-ried man __ to sing a wor-ried song; I'm wor-ried now, _____ but I won't be wor-ried long. _____

"Amen" is a spiritual. It can be harmonized with chords. The chords can be sung or played on the bells.

This bell part can be played with the first eight measures of the song.

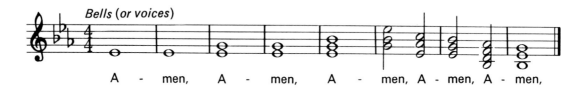

Amen

Spiritual
Arranged by Marion Downs

Find this chord in the bell part on page 122. This chord is said to be in **root position** because its lowest note is the chord root. What is the name of the chord?

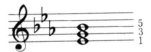

The notes of the chord above can also be arranged in this way.

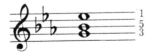

This chord arrangement is called an **inversion** because its root, E♭, is not at the bottom of the chord. Find this inversion in the bell part on page 122.

Build another inversion of the E♭ chord. Look at the bell part again to see whether your inversion is used.

Rolling Along

Words and music by Mary Val Marsh

I'll sing my song as I trav-el a-long, of my

home {
'neath the coun-try sky._____
on the moun-tain high._____
in the cit-y wide._____
} Oh, sing my

song as I trav-el a-long, As o-ver the road I

go._____ Sing-ing Roll-ee-o-long_____ I'm roll-ing,

Roll-ee-o-long_____ I'm roll-ing. Time to be

head-ing for home, So I'm just roll-ing,

roll-ing, I've got to be roll-ing a-long._____

Look at the chord names in "Rolling Along." Both number and letter names are used.

Chords are sometimes given number names. They are named for the position of the chord root in the scale.

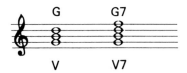

Sometimes a fourth tone is added to the V chord to make it more interesting. This tone is the interval of a seventh above the root. What is the name of the added note in the V7 chord below?

To accompany "Rolling Along," eleven people should each take a mallet and one bell from the C major scale. Use the bells from middle C up to the F an octave and a half above. Then practice playing the chords below.

I or C   = C   E   G
IV or F   = F   A   C
V7 or G7 = G   B   D   F

As the class sings the song, play the chords that are marked above the music. Play on each strong pulse, just as you would play the autoharp.

"New York City" is a song in traditional blues form. The blues form follows a standard harmonic pattern:

Phrase 1   I chord — 4 measures

Phrase 2   { IV chord — 2 measures
             I chord — 2 measures

Phrase 3   { V7 chord — 2 measures
             I chord — 2 measures

Syncopation is often found in a blues song. Where do you find syncopation in "New York City?"

New York City

Words and music by Joe Jaffe, Irwin Silber, Gladys Bashkin and Ernie Lieberman

Cloud-y in the west, looks like rain; I spent my last nick-el on a sub-way train in New York Cit-y, in New York Cit-y. In New York Cit-y, you real-ly got to know your line.

Play the accompaniment to "New York City" on the guitar, autoharp, or ukulele.

This blues song can be sung about any city or any town. Read the verse below. Then make up other verses to sing to this blues tune.

I looped the loop, I rocked and reeled,
I thought the Cubs played in Marshall Field
In the Windy City . . .

City Nights

When the lights of the city are bright and they gleam,
And the moon looks down on the level street,
I always dream of the selfsame dream;
Of hills that are wide and of woods that are green,
And of places where two brooks meet.

James Flexner

Collection, The Museum of Modern Art, New York. Blanchette Rockefeller Fund.

"Sanctuary" is circular in shape. The shape is not perfectly round like a ball, but it has a strong circular feeling. The outer shapes seem to move around the center and enclose it. The texture of the metal forms is rough; this roughness blends with the uneven edges of the individual shapes. Why do you think the artist who created this sculpture called it "Sanctuary"?

Not all blues are sung. Some are spoken. They are called "talking blues." Talking blues are often funny.

This is the "Original Talking Blues." Read the words with the rhythm shown until you have a real blues sound. Feel the syncopation as you read.

Original Talking Blues

Words by Lee Hays,
Fred Hellerman and Ronnie Gilbert

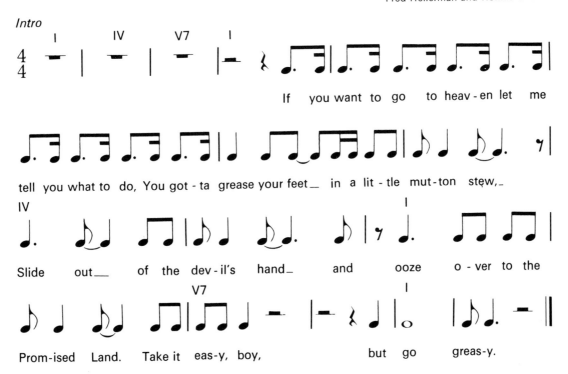

Accompany "Original Talking Blues" on the autoharp, guitar, or piano. Choose a key in which you can play easily. Use the standard blues pattern as a guide for changing the chords.

Make up your own talking blues and accompaniment.

Expression

Expression is vital to all art, for it is expression that communicates feeling. Artists who create a visual work, such as a painting or a wood carving, can build into their work any expression they wish. Creators of music or drama, however, cannot be sure how their work will be performed. Composers, of course, can indicate desired tempos (speed), dynamics (loud-soft), and articulation (how tones are begun and ended). They can also add other expressive words, such as "with dignity," "briskly," or "freely." It is the performers, however, who interpret the music according to their understanding and ideas.

Here are some frequently used terms and symbols of expression in music. Check to see how many of these you can identify. What other terms and symbols of expression in music do you know?,

Tempo	Dynamics	Articulation
allegro	*pp*	legato
largo	*f*	staccato
presto	decrescendo	

This song, which was popular during the American Revolution, is also known by the title "Buttermilk Hill." Its origin is the Irish ballad "Shule Aroon." Songs with similar words undoubtedly have been sung by people in every time and place in which loved ones have gone to war.

What expression can you use to interpret "Buttermilk Hill" effectively?

Johnny Has Gone for a Soldier

American Folk Song

"Tzena, Tzena" is a spirited Israeli folk song. It is often used for dancing. The verse and refrain can be sung together as a two-part song.

What expression terms and symbols on page 131 describe the way you think this song should be sung?

Tzena, Tzena

Words by Mitchell Parish
Music by Issachar Miron
and Julius Grossman

Verse

Tze - na, tze - na, tze - na, tze - na, hear the hap - py sounds of danc-ing,
Tze - na, tze - na, tze - na, tze - na, ev - 'ry-one can sing a - long, so

come _____ and dance a - long.
join _____ us in our song.

Refrain

La la la la, la la la la la la,

join us as we dance to - geth - er, sing - ing.

La la la la, la la la la la, come

join us in our hap - py song.

What effects have you seen that were produced by moonlight? Read this poem as expressively as you can. Then discuss how you used your voice to express the mood of the poem. You might work with others to create a musical setting in one of the following ways.

1. Choose appropriate background sounds. You might play the autoharp, percussion, or bells. (Try glissando effects or tones chosen at random.)

2. Choose some kind of scale (a mode, pentatonic scale, or a tone row) and create a melody for the words.

3. Work out a choral-speech performance for high, middle, and low-pitched speaking voices. Decide which lines or phrases should be spoken by each group of voices, or by individuals.

4. Combine suggestions 1 and 3.

The Night Will Never Stay

The night will never stay
The night will still go by,
Though with a million stars
You pin it to the sky;
Though you bind it with the blowing wind
And buckle it with the moon,
The night will slip away
Like sorrow or a tune.

Eleanor Farjeon

This song is often sung on patriotic holidays. It was written for the hundredth anniversary of the Declaration of Independence. It should be sung with great dignity and pride. What dynamics and tempo would you choose for interpreting this song?

God of Our Fathers

Music by George W. Warren
Words by D. C. Roberts
Arranged by M. V. M.

Descant (2nd verse only)

Thy love hath led us past,

Melody

1. God of our fa - thers, whose al - might-y hand
2. Thy love di - vine hath led us in the past,

In this land our lot is cast;

Leads forth in beau - ty all the star - ry band
In this free land by Thee our lot is cast;

Be our rul - er, guard-ian, guide, and stay.

Of shin - ing worlds in splen-dor through the skies,
Be Thou our rul - er, guard-ian, guide, and stay,

Thy word our chos - en way.

Our grate - ful songs be - fore Thy throne a - rise.
Thy word our law, Thy paths our chos - en way.

The structure of music

The structure of any object is its organization or the way in which it is put together.

Every object has an outer shape or form.

Every object also has inner parts which give that object its unique character.

Music also has an outer shape or plan. Each piece of music has many inner parts too, which fit together to create the whole composition. Music has both outer and inner structure or form.

The structure of a work of art is determined by the way in which shapes, colors, lines, and textures are organized. The artist Raoul Dufy repeats shapes, colors, and lines in his painting. He also uses a variety of sizes to provide visual interest to the picture.

137

Inside the music

How would you begin to build a piece of music? You might start with a rhythmic **motif,** or idea.

You might start with a melodic motif.

Perhaps you would begin with some lines of poetry, or with an idea for a story.

"Morning comes early..."

Morning Comes Early

Slovak Folk Song
Words Adapted

1. Morn-ing comes ear-ly, the sun's so bright;
2. Come then, my com-rade, to greet the day;

Do not lie sleep-ing when all is light.
Here we are wait-ing, do not de-lay.

No time to waste now, Get up in haste now,
Hur-ry a-long now, Join us in song now,

Time to be work-ing, then rest at night.
Sing-ing will drive all our cares a-way.

How many times do you find this rhythmic motif in "Morning Comes Early"?

Where is the motif changed so that the melody becomes more interesting?

139

In the old West, the cattle drive to the railroad was long and hard. Sometimes it took several weeks. The cowboys often had to drive the cattle over rough trails and through patches of thick, thorny bushes called chaparral. The cowboys were glad when they saw the railroad corral, for this meant the end of the cattle drive was in sight.

The Railroad Corral

Cowboy Song

1. We're up in the morn - ing ere break - ing of day,
2. Come take up your cinch - es, come shake out your reins,
3. The af - ter - noon sha - dows are start - ing to lean,

The chuck wag - on's bus - y, the flap - jack's in play.
Come wake your old bron - co and break for the plains;
When the chuck wag - on sticks in the marsh - y ra - vine;

The herd is a - stir o - ver hill - side and vale,
Come roust out your steers from the long chap - ar - ral,
The herds scat - ter far - ther than vi - sion can look,

With the night rid - ers crowd - ing them in - to the trail.
For the out - fit is off to the rail - road cor - ral.
You can bet all true punch - ers will help out the cook.

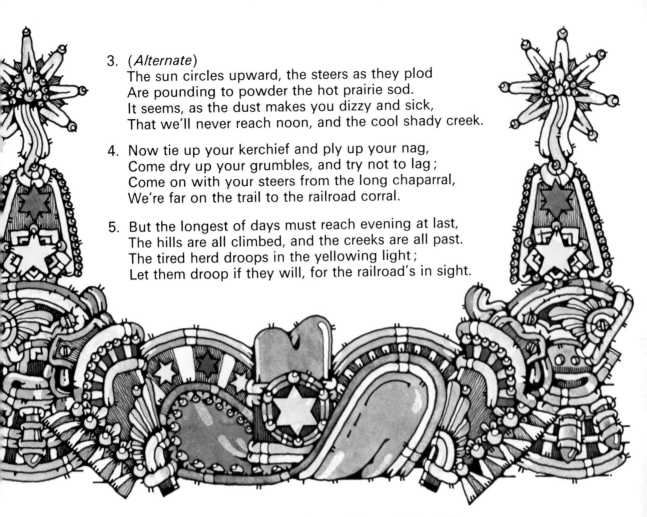

3. (*Alternate*)
   The sun circles upward, the steers as they plod
   Are pounding to powder the hot prairie sod.
   It seems, as the dust makes you dizzy and sick,
   That we'll never reach noon, and the cool shady creek.

4. Now tie up your kerchief and ply up your nag,
   Come dry up your grumbles, and try not to lag;
   Come on with your steers from the long chaparral,
   We're far on the trail to the railroad corral.

5. But the longest of days must reach evening at last,
   The hills are all climbed, and the creeks are all past.
   The tired herd droops in the yellowing light;
   Let them droop if they will, for the railroad's in sight.

How many times is this rhythmic motif used in "The Railroad Corral"?

How many times is this motif used?

Find two phrases with exactly the same rhythm. Find another phrase in which the rhythm is varied slightly.

Which phrase has a very different rhythmic structure?

141

Varying a musical idea

A musical idea may be as small as a motif, or as large as an entire song. There are many ways of developing a musical idea into a complete piece of music. There must be enough repetition to unify the music, and enough variation to make it interesting.

Here is a musical idea. It is the first phrase of the song "Yankee Doodle."

This phrase has been treated in four different ways. Discover what has been done in each example.

The first phrase of "Yankee Doodle" was treated in the following ways. Which change was made in each example?

augmentation   doubling the duration of notes in a melody

altered tones   changing some of the pitches of a melody

extension   adding notes to make a melody longer

ornamentation   adding new tones within a melody

Here is a phrase of "Island in the Sun," page 82. Vary it in one of the four ways listed above. Write your phrase on music paper or on the chalkboard. Play it on the recorder, bells, or piano. Let other students discover how you have varied the phrase.

Collection, The Museum of Modern Art, New York, Mrs. Simon Guggenheim Fund.

In art, repetition of visual ideas can be important in building a structure. In "Still Life with Three Puppies," Gauguin has organized shapes in groups of three. How many groups of three can you find in the painting? What else is repeated to create unity in the painting? Sketch your own arrangement of small groups of objects. Then make a painting from your sketch. Decide how you will unify your painting.

This hiking song from Germany may be familiar to you. The descant sounds something like an Alpine yodel. Part of this descant was written by a sixth-grade student.

Holla Hi, Holla Ho

German Folk Song

We will leave this morn, Hol-la hi, hol-la ho! Hol-la hi, hol-la ho!

We will leave in the ear-ly morn, Hol-la hi! Hol-la ho!

Come back when light's gone, hol-la ho! Hol-la ho!

Then come back when the day-light's gone, Hol-la, hol-la ho!

Where do you find rhythmic augmentation in the melody of "Holla Hi, Holla Ho"?

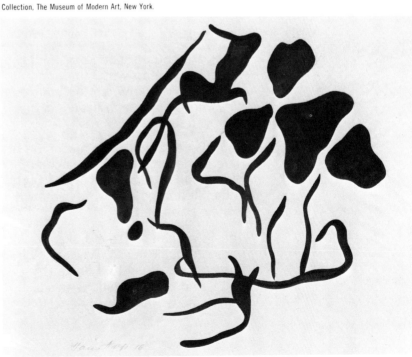

In "Automatic Drawing," Jean Arp used only shapes and lines. The picture has a strong feeling of unity. The lines are curved and similar in thickness. The shapes are rounded. The lines and shapes are close together to suggest a rectangular, slanting form.

A crawdad looks like a small lobster and lives in warm-water streams. Another name for a crawdad is "crayfish."

The Crawdad Song

American Folk Song

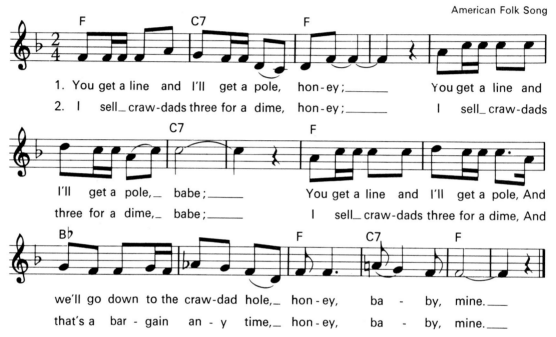

1. You get a line and I'll get a pole, hon-ey;_____ You get a line and
2. I sell_ craw-dads three for a dime, hon-ey;_____ I sell_ craw-dads

I'll get a pole,_ babe;_____ You get a line and I'll get a pole, And
three for a dime,_ babe;_____ I sell_ craw-dads three for a dime, And

we'll go down to the craw-dad hole,_ hon-ey, ba - by, mine.___
that's a bar - gain an - y time,_ hon-ey, ba - by, mine.___

3. What will you do when the pond runs dry, honey?
   What will you do when the pond runs dry, babe?
   What will you do when the pond runs dry?
   I'll sit right down and have a cry,
   Honey, baby, mine.

4. Here comes a man with a sack on his back, honey;
   Here comes a man with a sack on his back, babe;
   Here comes a man with a sack on his back,
   Totin' all the crawdads he can pack,
   Honey, baby, mine.

5. I heard a duck say to a drake, honey;
   I heard a duck say to a drake, babe;
   I heard a duck say to a drake,
   You'll find no crawdads in this lake,
   Honey, baby, mine.

"The Crawdad Song" is a folk song. Folk singers often change folk songs to suit their individual styles. This version of "The Crawdad Song" has an altered tone in it. Where is it?

Create your own version of this song or another folk song. Try altered tones, augmentation, syncopation, and other kinds of pitch and rhythmic variation.

Artists often repeat a line, shape, or color as an answer to or an echo of a more prominent visual idea. Look at the Indian blanket. The red zig-zag lines in the middle are edged with black. This outline is repeated in white as an echo.

Notice how the repeated diamond shapes provide rhythm and unity.

Weave or paint a composition based on a pattern of your own design. Repeat this pattern with variations throughout the whole piece.

The Snake

A snake! Though it passes,
eyes that had glared at me
stay in the grasses.

Kyoshi

Snakes

Words by Larry Lo Presti
Music by Ronald Lo Presti

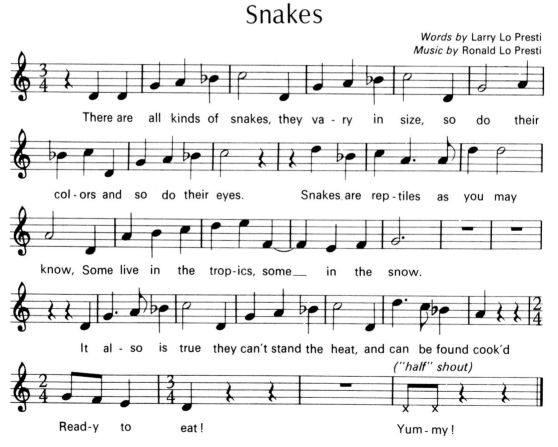

There are all kinds of snakes, they va-ry in size, so do their

col-ors and so do their eyes. Snakes are rep-tiles as you may

know, Some live in the trop-ics, some___ in the snow.

It al-so is true they can't stand the heat, and can be found cook'd

("half" shout)

Read-y to eat! Yum-my!

148

This is the basic motif used in the song "Snakes."

How many times do you find this motif, or a variation of it, in the song?

In what ways did the composer vary the motif? What keeps the song from becoming monotonous?

Make a design or picture based on a snake motif. You might want to look at pictures of snakes to get some ideas of their forms, colors, and patterns. Make a drawing in black and white, using con- *trast to make the designs stand out clearly. Make another drawing in color. Remember that variety can be achieved by changing the size of a basic shape as you repeat it.*

Look at the descant. What two notes are used? Where
is the descant syncopated?

Little David, Play on Your Harp

Afro-American Spiritual
Arranged by Mary Val Marsh

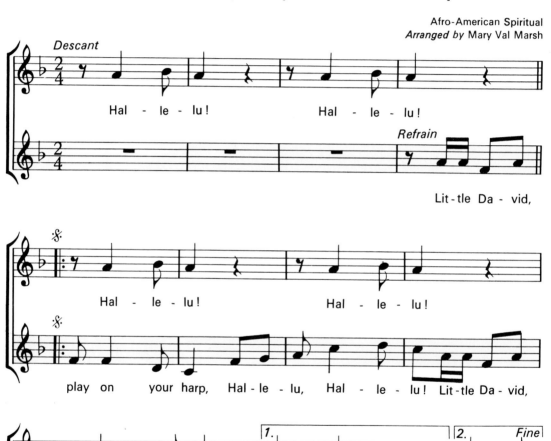

The following signs appear in this song. Find the signs in the music. Explain the meaning of each sign.

Musical questions and answers

The words in the verse of "Vreneli" ask and answer questions. The melody does this too. What causes the melody at the end of the boys' phrase to sound like a question? What makes the girls' second phrase sound like an answer?

Vreneli

Swiss Folk Song

Boys: "Oh, Vren - e - li, my pret - ty one, pray tell me, where's your home?"

Girls: "My home, it is in Swit - zer - land, 'Tis made of wood and stone;

My home it is in Swit - zer - land, 'Tis made of wood and stone."

Refrain

Girls: Yo ho ho, tra la la la, Yo ho ho, tra la la la. Yo ho ho, tra la la la,

Boys: Yo ho ho, Yo ho ho, Yo ho ho,

Yo ho ho, tra la la la. Yo ho ho, tra la la la, Yo ho ho tra la la la.

Yo ho ho,   Yo ho ho,   Yo ho ho,

Yo ho ho,   tra   la   la   la.   Yo ho ho!

Yo ho ho,   Yo   ho.   Yo   ho!

A full cadence is an ending that sounds finished. **A half cadence** is an ending that seems to ask a question. Is a full cadence like a musical question or an answer? Where are the full cadences in the verse of this song?

The term "folk art" is used to identify art created by groups of people to make their furniture, homes, and other buildings more interesting to look at. The Pennsylvania Dutch used free-flowing lines, bright colors, and symbols such as the tulip and the bird.

Make a design of your own, using this kind of style, to decorate something you use or see every day. You may wish to use your design to illustrate a familiar song.

The melody of "Ifca's Castle" has a very simple construction. The first four measures go up in pitch, as if to ask a question. This rise in pitch produces a certain amount of **tension.** The next four measures go down in pitch, and seem to provide an answer. This causes a feeling of **release** from the tension. Most music is constructed to create some feelings of tension and release.

This song is about an ancient castle standing near a river in Czechoslovakia. The song is a round. It may be sung by as many as eight groups.

Ifca's Castle

Czech Folk Song

1. A - bove a plain of gold and green A young boy's head is clear-ly seen.

2. But no, 'tis not his lift - ing head, 'Tis If - ca's cas - tle spires in - stead.

Refrain

A - hu - ya, hu - ya, hu - ya - ya, Swift-ly flow-ing wa - ter,

A - hu - ya, hu - ya, hu - ya - ya, Swift - ly flow - ing wa - ter.

A Song of the Open Air

Sicilian Folk Song
Words by Janet E. Tobitt

Melody: Come out, the sun is high, the wind is fair;____

Harmony: Come out,____ the wind____ is fair;____

Come out and join_ us in the o - pen air.____

Come join us in the o - pen air.____

Come out, the sun is high, the wind is fair;____

Come out,____ the wind____ is fair;____

Find a phrase in the melody of this song where most of the pitches go up. Find a phrase in which most of the pitches go down. Which phrase seems to create tension? What effect does the other phrase have?

This Mexican song of greeting is usually sung at dawn. Although it is a morning song, it can also be a birthday song. Harmony in thirds is often found in many Mexican folk songs.

Morning Song
(Las Mañanitas)

Mexican Folk Song
Translated by Olcutt and Phyllis Sanders
Based on an English text by Janet E. Tobitt

With a morn-ing song we greet you As King Da-vid used to sing,
Es-tas son las ma-ña-ni-tas Que can-ta-ba el Rey Da-vid,

But his song was not as love-ly As is the mu-sic we bring.
Pe-ro no e-ran tan bo-ni-tas Co-mo las can-tan a-quí.

A-wake, then, O my be-lov-ed, A-wake, for the dawn is nigh;
Des-pier-ta, mi bien, des-pier-ta, Mi-ra que ya a-ma-ne-ció;

Now the birds are sweet-ly sing-ing, The moon has gone from the sky.
Ya las pa-ja-ri-llos can-tan, La lu-na ya se o-cul-tó.

To use "Morning Song" as a birthday song, sing these words in the last phrase of the verse.

And since now it is your birthday,
To you this music we bring.

Por ser día de tu santo
Te las cantamos a ti.

Where are the full cadences in this song? Can you find half cadences?

Which kind of cadence is created by musical tension? Which by release from tension?

The forms of music

All music has an outer shape or form.

There are very short forms of music, such as a three-part (A B A) song or instrumental piece, or a simple round.

There are also longer forms of music.

theme and variations

rondo

suite

symphony

concerto

opera

oratorio

Which of these terms do you recognize? Which forms are for instruments and which forms are for voices and instruments? What else do you know about these forms of music?

Works of art organized in an irregular way have <u>informal balance</u>. These objects have unity, yet one cannot divide them into equal halves. The wood carving, "Virgin and Child," made in France in the 1200's, has informal balance. The figure of the Mother gives an impression of formal balance. However, the Child on the knee and the placement of the Mother's left hand makes the organization informal. Describe the feeling of this work.

Phrase form

"The Rose" is one of many German folk tunes arranged by Johannes Brahms. Brahms was one of the great composers of the Romantic Age in music (about 1825–1900). He wrote and arranged music for both voices and instruments. Listen to the Brahms arrangement on the recording.

The Rose

German Folk Song
Words by Martha Aldredge

How love-ly the ros-es that bloom by your gar-den wall;

Their frag-rant per-fume lin-gers soft o-ver___ all.

Sweet maid-en now I beg of you to pick one blos-som fair,

To re-mind me of your beau-ty, with which it can-not com-pare.

Music is often built by putting phrases together in very regular ways. For example, many folk songs have an even number of phrases, with an equal number of measures in each. One or two phrases may be repeated, resulting in phrase forms such as these.

A B A B   A A B A   A B A C

Often there is a slight variation in one of the repeated phrases. The variation is indicated by the prime mark ('). A A' B B' or A B A B'.

"The Rose" is a song with regular phrase form. How many measures are there in each phrase of the song? Which of the following letter groups describes the form of the song?

A B A B   A A B A   A B A C

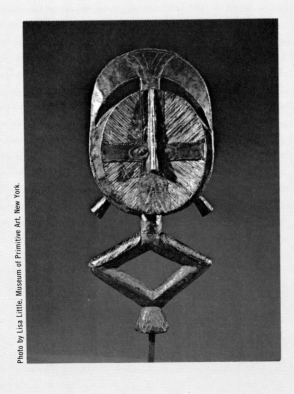

The organization of a work of art can be either regular or irregular. Works of primitive art and folk art often have a regular organization. The "Bakota Figure" from Gabon, Africa, is organized in a regular way. You could draw a line down the center of the figure and each side would be the same. This type of organization is called <u>formal balance</u>. Formal balance communicates feelings of dignity.

Sing a Rainbow

Words and music by Arthur Hamilton
Arranged by Mary Val Marsh

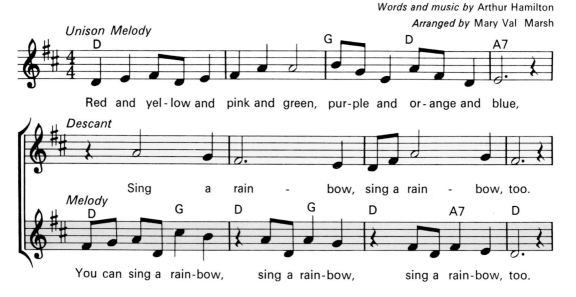

Unison Melody

Red and yel-low and pink and green, pur-ple and or-ange and blue,

Descant

Sing a rain - bow, sing a rain - bow, too.

Melody

You can sing a rain-bow, sing a rain-bow, sing a rain-bow, too.

Lis-ten with your eyes, lis-ten with your eyes; and sing ev-'ry-thing you see.

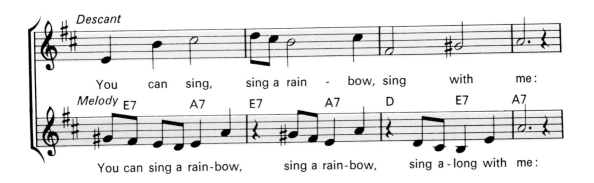

You can sing, sing a rain - bow, sing with me:

You can sing a rain-bow, sing a rain-bow, sing a-long with me:

Red and yel-low and pink and green, pur-ple and or-ange and blue,

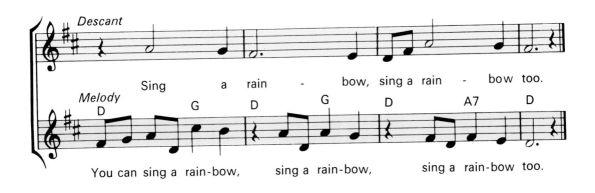

Sing a rain - bow, sing a rain - bow too.

You can sing a rain-bow, sing a rain-bow, sing a rain-bow too.

This song has six phrases of four measures each, but the form is somewhat unusual. What is the phrase form of the melody?

165

"Passing Through Lorraine" is an old French marching song. Lorraine was a province of France. It was in Lorraine that Joan of Arc, the great French heroine, was born. The Cross of Lorraine is the French battle emblem.

Passing Through Lorraine

(En Passant par la Lorraine)

French Folk Song

1. Through Lor - raine I went a - walk-ing in my wood -en shoes;____
1. En pas - sant par la Lor - rai - ne A - vec mes sa - bots;____

Through Lor - raine I went a - walk -ing in my wood-en shoes;____
En pas - sant par la Lor - rai - ne A - vec mes sa - bots;____

When to my sur - prise I saw them — sol - diers three were watch - ing
Ren - con - trai trois ca - pi - tai - nes, A - vec mes sa - bots, don-

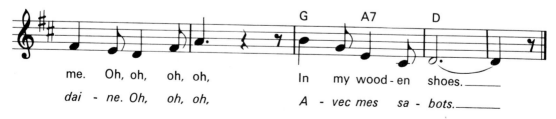

me. Oh, oh, oh, oh, In my wood - en shoes. ____
dai - ne. Oh, oh, oh, A - vec mes sa - bots. ____

2. Then they laughed and called me ugly in my wooden shoes;
   Then they laughed and called me ugly in my wooden shoes;
   But I said I was not ugly in my wooden shoes, not ugly,
   Oh, oh, oh, In my wooden shoes.

2. *Ils m'ont appelée vilaine, avec mes sabots;*
   Ils m'ont appelée vilaine, avec mes sabots;
   Je ne suis pas si vilaine, avec mes sabots, dondaine.
   Oh, oh, oh, Avec mes sabots.

3. Tell me, if I were so ugly in my wooden shoes,
   Tell me, if I were so ugly in my wooden shoes,
   Would the Prince have said he loves me, in my wooden
      shoes, he loves me?
   Oh, oh, oh, In my wooden shoes.

3. *Je ne suis pas si vilaine, avec mes sabots;*
   Je ne suis pas si vilaine, avec mes sabots;
   Puisque le fils du roi m'aime, avec mes sabots, dondaine.
   Oh, oh, oh, Avec mes sabots.

Some of the most interesting music contains phrases of different lengths or has an uneven number of phrases. The song "Passing Through Lorraine" has 16 measures. The first two phrases have 4 measures each.

$\frac{1}{2}$ measure   1 measure   1 measure   1 measure $\frac{1}{2}$ measure

But the third phrase does not stop after 4 measures. It is $5\frac{1}{2}$ measures long. A short phrase of $2\frac{1}{2}$ measures ends the song. This song has an **irregular phrase form** because the phrases have different lengths.

167

On Watching the Construction of a Skyscraper

Nothing sings from these orange trees,
Rindless steel as smooth as supling skin,
Except a crane's brief wheeze
And all the muffled, clanking din
Of rivets nosing in like bees.

Burton Raffel

There are many ballads that tell tall tales about real or imaginary heroes of the past. You may know songs about John Henry, the hero of the rails, or Paul Bunyan, the lumberjack. Joe Magarac was a legendary steel mill worker.

Is the phrase form of this song regular or irregular?

Joe Magarac

Words and music by
Jacob A. Evanson

1. I'll tell you a-bout a steel_____ man,
2. He was sired in the moun-tain by red iron ore,
3. His should-ers are as big as the steel mill door,
4. With his hands he can break a half-a-ton dol-ly,

Joe Ma - ga - rac, that's the man!

168

I'll tell you a-bout a steel_____ man,
He was sired in the moun-tain by red iron ore,
His shoul-ders are as big as the steel mill door,
With his hands he can break a half-a-ton dol-ly,

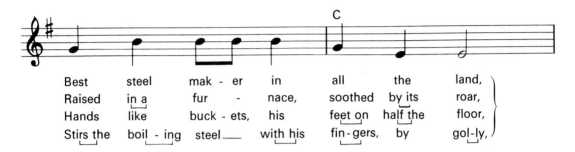

Best steel mak-er in all the land,
Raised in a fur - nace, soothed by its roar,
Hands like buck-ets, his feet on half the floor,
Stirs the boil-ing steel_ with his fin-gers, by gol-ly,

Steel - heart Ma - ga - rac, that's the man!

5. He grabs the cooling steel—his hands like wringers,
Joe Magarac, that's the man!
And makes eight rails between his ten fingers.
Steel-heart Magarac, that's the man!

6. Joe can walk on the furnace rim,
Joe Magarac, that's the man!
From furnace to furnace—just a step for him.
Steel-heart Magarac, that's the man!

7. Joe never sleeps, but he's got to eat,
Joe Magarac, that's the man!
Hot steel soup, cold ingots for meat.
Steel-heart Magarac, that's the man!

8. Now, if you think this man's not real,
Joe Magarac, that's the man!
Then jump in a furnace, see him cook the steel.
Steel-heart Magarac, that's the man!

A five-part round is rather unusual. The form of "Come and Sing" is irregular.

Come and Sing

Swedish Round
Words by Sarah Jacobson

Come now and sing, And let your voi - ces ring.

A song can make your trou - bles light - er,

hap - pi - ness it soon will bring. Come now and sing.

Poetry, as well as music, may be written in either regular or irregular phrase form. Here are two poems about winter. Both have descriptive words to paint a picture of winter's beauty. Think about the word pictures as you read the poems. Decide which poem has an irregular phrase form.

New Snow

The pines are white-powdered,
  Delicately tossed
With fairy filigrees
  Of silver frost.

The top of the mountain
  Is lost in a cloud,
While the world is silent
  And the wind unloud.

Drink in the beauty,
  The shadows . . . the glow . . .
The wonder of winter
  And the new white snow!

Catharine Bryant Rowles

Walk on a Winter Day

Come walk with me,
  And we shall pass
Silent as shadows
  Over the grass.

We shall walk beneath
A slender fairy tree
  Whose branches hold
The buds of snow,
  The silver apples of the cold.

We shall speak no word
As we go,
But we shall hear the bird
That nests in the fairy tree
Singing a winter song
For you and me.

Sara Van Alstyne Allen

"The Green Bushes" and "One Morn in May" are two songs that are alike in some ways and different in others. Both songs deal with the same subject. Both songs have four phrases.

Listen to the recording; then look at the music. How many differences are there in the melodies of the two songs? Here are some clues.

meter   scale   phrase form

The Green Bushes

Old English Song
Adapted

1. As___ I was a - walk - ing one morn - ing in May,
2. "Oh,___ why are you wait - ing here, my pret - ty maid?"

To hear the birds whis - tle and see the lambs play,
"I'm a - wait - ing my true love," so soft - ly she said.

I___ spied a young maid - en, so sweet - ly sang she,
"Let__ me be your true love, and please do a - gree,

Down by the green bush - es, where she chanced to meet me.
Down by the green bush - es, to_____ mar - ry with me."

One Morn in May

Words and music by
Phyllis Simpson

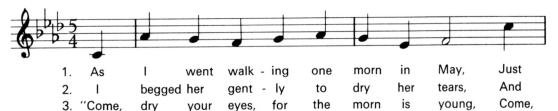

1. As I went walk - ing one morn in May, Just
2. I begged her gent - ly to dry her tears, And
3. "Come, dry your eyes, for the morn is young, Come,

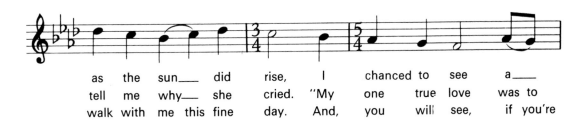

as the sun___ did rise, I chanced to see a___
tell me why___ she cried. "My one true love was to
walk with me this fine day. And, you will see, if you're

love - ly maid with tear - drops in_____ her eyes.
meet me here, but now I fear_____ he lied."
pleased with me, your tears will soon go a - way."

Do the measures of five metric beats in this song seem to divide into subsets of 2 + 3 (count 1 2, 1 2 3) or subsets of 3 + 2 (count 1 2 3, 1 2)?

`LISTENING` *Take Five*
Dave Brubeck

"Take Five" is written in $\frac{5}{4}$ meter. Listen to find out whether the subsets in "Take Five" are the same as in the song "One Morn in May."

Come and Sing Together

Hungarian Canon
Words by Max T. Krone

1. If you'd dance, then you must have boots of shin - ing leath - er,
2. If you'd wed a pret - ty girl, that will cost you mon - ey;
3. If you want an - oth - er verse, how could we be know - ing?

Mon - ey in your pock - et - book, in your cap a feath - er.
She will want a hun - dred things, rain - y days or sun - ny!
Why not make up one your - self, Just to keep it go - ing?

But if you would sing with me,
But if you would sing with me,
Mu - sic is for ev - 'ry one!

You don't need a cent, you see, so come and sing to - geth - er!
You don't need a cent, you see, so come and sing to - geth - er!
You can have a lot of fun, so come and sing to - geth - er!

If you'd dance, then you must have boots of shin - ing leath - er!
If you'd wed a pret - ty girl, that will cost you mon - ey!
Try a verse you made your - self, then just keep it go - ing! Oh!

174

"Come and Sing Together" is built in a very interesting way. Test yourself to see how much you know about musical structure.

1. How many phrases are in the song?
2. Which phrases of the melody are exactly alike?
3. What letters would you use to show the phrase form?
4. In what ways is the phrase form irregular?
5. What happens to the rhythm in phrases 3 and 4?
6. What would you call the last measure that is to be sung only at the end of the last verse?

USING MUSICAL PHRASES

Create your own music. Here are two phrases of melody.
Play them on an instrument, then sing them.

Use these phrases to build a longer melody. Here are some
ideas for developing your music.

Repeat one or both of these phrases.

Add new phrases of your own.

Repeat any part of a phrase.

Create a variation of a phrase.

Try different ideas until you are satisfied with your music.
Add words to your melody to make a song.

Does your song have a regular or an irregular form?

Does your song seem balanced?

Does your song end with a full cadence?

Artists often begin a work without knowing how it will end. Their ideas develop as they work. Sometimes a chance encounter with stones or driftwood on a beach, or a cloud formation may give the artist an idea for a new work. The random scribbled lines in Figure I were developed into the picture of the fish which you see in Figure 2.

You too can use this idea. Draw some random lines on a piece of paper with a crayon or pencil. Then look at it to see whether the lines make anything —fish, animal, flower, tree, or person? Keep turning the paper until the marks suggest something to you. Change the lines and shapes to complete your picture. Use the principles of unity and variety to achieve a well-balanced structure in your picture.

Theme and variations

The Shakers were religious people who first settled in New England. They were called "Shaking Quakers" because they showed their religious feelings through singing, dancing, and moving.

"Simple Gifts" is one of the most popular of all Shaker songs. The words express the Shakers' belief in the importance of leading a simple life.

Simple Gifts

Shaker Song

'Tis the gift to be sim-ple, 'tis the gift to be free, 'Tis the gift to come down where we ought to be, And when we find our-selves in the place just right, 'Twill be in the val - ley of love and de - light. When true sim - pli - ci - ty is gained, To

bow and to bend we shan't be a-shamed, To turn, turn will

be our de-light, Till by turn-ing, turn-ing we come round right.

LISTENING *Appalachian Spring, excerpt*
Aaron Copland

The well-known American composer, Aaron Copland, used the tune "Simple Gifts" as the theme in a section of a ballet. The ballet *Appalachian Spring* is about life in a rural community in the Appalachian mountains of Pennsylvania. The Shakers sang "Simple Gifts" in a lively manner. Aaron Copland used the song for a calm scene in the ballet.

The melody is heard in five variations in this section of the ballet. Listen to discover in what order the following variations are heard.

full orchestral harmony

solo statement of the theme, with light accompaniment

duet in thirds

high brasses playing melody, with harmony often played in fourths

melody in low instruments, using some imitation, with an ostinato-type accompaniment in higher instruments

179

Cindy

Appalachian Folk Song
Arranged by Mary Val Marsh

Descant

1. ... an ap-ple a - hang-ing on a
2. .... she loved me, she called me sug-ar
3. .... a nee-dle as fine as I could

Melody F   C7

1. I wish I was an ap-ple a - hang-ing on a tree, And
2. She told me that she loved me, She called me sug-ar plum, She
3. I wish I had a nee-dle, as fine as I could sew, I'd

tree, So Cin - dy'd take a bite of me!
plum, And then I thought my time had come.
sew, With that gal down the road I'd go!

F   Bb   G   F   Bb   F   **Refrain**

ev - 'ry time my Cin - dy passed, she'd take a bite of me!
threw her arms a - round me and I thought my time had come. Get a-long
sew that gal to my coat-tail, and down the road I'd go!

Get a-long home, Cin - dy, Get a-long home, Cin - dy,

Bb   F

home, Cin - dy, Cin-dy, get a-long home, Cin - dy, Cin-dy, Get a-long

First sing only the melody of "Cindy." Accompany it on an autoharp, guitar, banjo, ukulele, or piano.

Which of these words are sung at full cadences?

| tree | me | Cindy | day |

What kind of chord usually occurs at a full cadence? What kind of chord would you not choose for a full cadence?

LISTENING   *"Cindy" from* KENTUCKY MOUNTAIN PORTRAITS
Lyndol Mitchell

Listen to this musical portrait of Cindy. How does this music seem to describe the woman in the song?

Composers often use a folk melody as the basis for a larger composition. Here are some of the devices by which a composer may develop a simple melody into a longer composition. Which terms do you understand?

introduction   change in melodic   change of key
                 rhythm

tempo change   octave displacement   change of meter
ornamentation   change of instrumen- volume change
imitation   tation   extension

Listen again to the musical portrait of Cindy. Which of the devices above did the composer use?

181

Here is the melody of a song you may know. Play it on
the bells to find out the name of the song.

Make a variation of your own, using one or more of
the devices in the list on page 181. Write your variation on music paper or record it. Play or sing your
variation for the class.

Dream Variation

To fling my arms wide
In some place of the sun,
To whirl and to dance
Till the white day is done.
Then rest at cool evening
Beneath a tall tree
While night comes on gently,
   Dark like me—
That is my dream!

To fling my arms wide
In the face of the sun,
Dance! Whirl! Whirl!
Till the quick day is done.
Rest at pale evening . . .
A tall, slim tree . . .
Night coming tenderly
   Black like me.

Langston Hughes

The symphony

A **symphony** is a composition that usually consists of three or four large parts called movements. The first great composers of symphonies were Haydn and Mozart. The musical period in which they lived is sometimes called the Classical Age (about 1750–1825). During this time, the symphony developed as one of the major forms of music. In the Classical Age a symphony usually contained four movements, in this order.

Allegro (fast)   Adagio (slow) or Andante (moderate)

Minuet (a dance-like movement)   Allegro (fast)

Each movement of a symphony has an individual form.

LISTENING *Symphony No. 94, Movements 2 and 4 Franz Joseph Haydn*

The "Surprise" symphony by Franz Joseph Haydn is one of the best-known symphonies from the Classical Age. Haydn wrote 104 symphonies and many other works. Listen for the surprises in the second movement. Haydn is said to have planned them to waken the nobles of the court, who often dozed during performances.

CAREERS

© Ben Ross

A **conductor** leads musical groups in performing. Before beginning rehearsals, the conductor prepares the score to reflect his or her interpretation of the work for an expressive performance. Conductors need to be skilled musicians and leaders.

Here is the "A" part of the theme of the Andante movement.

How do the pitches of the first two measures move? The next two measures?

Play the theme on piano, bells, or another instrument. Sing the theme.

Here is the "B" part of the theme.

The Andante movement of this symphony is written in theme and variation form. First Haydn states the theme as follows: A A B B. Then he presents four variations, followed by a coda, or short ending. These are the variations, in scrambled order.

- change to minor key
- addition of countermelody
- full orchestra, with much ornamentation
- oboe melody; then oboe and flute duet at the same time as the melody in the strings

Listen to the second movement of *Symphony No. 94.* Write the four variations in the order in which you hear them, following the statement of the theme.

The short fourth movement of *Symphony No. 94* has only two themes. The main theme returns again and again. What instruments begin this theme?

Music, drama, and dance: The opera

An **opera** is a play told through acting, singing, and instrumental music. The **dialogue** (conversation) in an opera is usually sung. In some operas, part of the conversation is spoken. *H.M.S. Pinafore* uses spoken conversations and songs to tell a story. Because it is short and humorous, it is called a **light opera** or an **operetta.** Two people worked together to create *H.M.S. Pinafore.* Sir William S. Gilbert wrote the story and the words of the songs. Sir Arthur Sullivan composed the music. A short version of *H.M.S. Pinafore* is presented here for you to read and sing. The entire class may sing the songs. After you have sung and listened to the music, you may wish to perform it as a musical play. When this is done, the readers will not be needed.

Carl Schofield from Rapho Guillumette Pictures, Inc., New York.

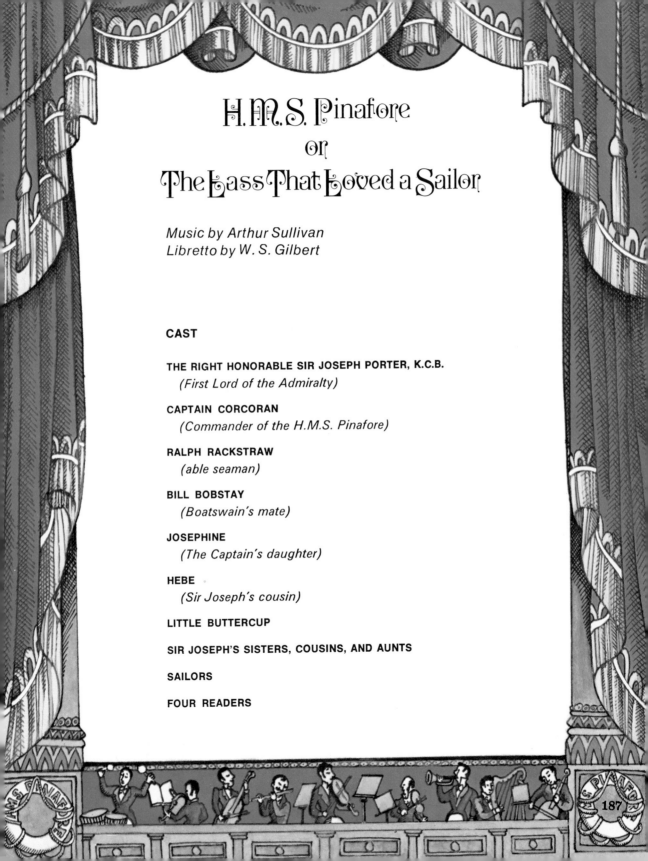

H.M.S. Pinafore
or
The Lass That Loved a Sailor

Music by Arthur Sullivan
Libretto by W. S. Gilbert

CAST

THE RIGHT HONORABLE SIR JOSEPH PORTER, K.C.B.
  (First Lord of the Admiralty)

CAPTAIN CORCORAN
  (Commander of the H.M.S. Pinafore)

RALPH RACKSTRAW
  (able seaman)

BILL BOBSTAY
  (Boatswain's mate)

JOSEPHINE
  (The Captain's daughter)

HEBE
  (Sir Joseph's cousin)

LITTLE BUTTERCUP

SIR JOSEPH'S SISTERS, COUSINS, AND AUNTS

SAILORS

FOUR READERS

This story takes place aboard a ship of the British Navy called *H.M.S. Pinafore*. The ship is docked at an English port. The sailors are splicing rope and cleaning the deck. As they work, Little Buttercup comes aboard to sell food and trinkets to the sailors.

I'm Called Little Buttercup

Buttercup

I'm called Lit - tle But - ter - cup, Dear Lit - tle But - ter - cup,
Then buy of your But - ter - cup, Dear Lit - tle But - ter - cup,

Though I could nev - er tell why; But still I'm called But - ter - cup,
Sail - ors should nev - er be shy; So buy of your But - ter - cup,

Poor Lit - tle But - ter - cup, Sweet Lit - tle But - ter - cup I.
Poor Lit - tle But - ter - cup, Come, of your But - ter - cup buy.

I've snuff and to - bac - cy, and ex - cel - lent jack - y; I've scis - sors and
I've rib - bons and lac - es to set off the fac - es of

watch - es and knives; pret - ty young sweet - hearts and wives.

188

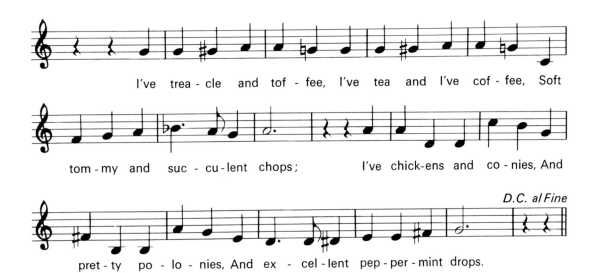

I've trea - cle and tof - fee, I've tea and I've cof - fee, Soft tom - my and suc - cu - lent chops; I've chick - ens and co - nies, And

D.C. al Fine

pret - ty po - lo - nies, And ex - cel - lent pep - per - mint drops.

READER 2

Dick Deadeye, an unpopular member of the crew, pushes his way through the sailors. They all pull away from him.

LITTLE BUTTERCUP

What's the matter with the man? Isn't he well?

BILL BOBSTAY

Don't take no heed of him. That's only poor Dick Deadeye.

READER 1

Ralph Rackstraw, one of the sailors, enters. He looks very sad.

LITTLE BUTTERCUP

And who is this?

BILL BOBSTAY

That is the smartest lad in all the fleet, Ralph Rackstraw!

LITTLE BUTTERCUP

Ralph! That name. So sad!

Ralph tells the crew why he is so sad. He is in love with the Captain's daughter. He knows it is hopeless. The crew tries to convince him that he is wrong in courting her. She can have nothing to do with a common sailor. Captain Corcoran enters, causing the argument to stop.

I Am the Captain of the Pinafore

sea! What nev-er? No nev-er! What nev-er?_ Hard-ly

ev-er! He's hard-ly ev-er sick at sea! Then give three cheers, and

one cheer more, For the har-dy cap-tain of the Pin-a-fore! Then

give three cheers, and one cheer more, For the cap-tain of the Pin-a-fore!

READER 4

The crew leaves Captain Corcoran alone.

LITTLE BUTTERCUP

Sir, you are sad. Tell me. I will understand. I am a mother!

CAPTAIN CORCORAN

Yes, Little Buttercup, I am sad. Sir Joseph wishes to marry my daughter, Josephine, but she does not seem interested.

LITTLE BUTTERCUP

Ah, I understand all too well. But look! Here comes your daughter now.

CAPTAIN CORCORAN

My child, I am sad to see you looking in such low spirits. You should look your best today. Sir Joseph will be here this afternoon.

JOSEPHINE

Father, I cannot love him! I love someone else!

CAPTAIN CORCORAN

Who is it?

JOSEPHINE

He is but a humble sailor on board your own ship.

CAPTAIN CORCORAN

Impossible!

JOSEPHINE

It is true, too true.

CAPTAIN CORCORAN

Come, child. We must talk this over. I hold little value in rank or wealth, but the line must be drawn somewhere.

READER 1

Sir Joseph's boat approaches the ship. He is accompanied by the admiring crowd of sisters, cousins, and aunts that go with him wherever he goes.

READER 2

The sailors all greet Sir Joseph and his relatives.

CAPTAIN CORCORAN

Now, give three cheers!

SAILORS

Hurrah! Hurrah! Hurrah!

I Am the Monarch of the Sea

Sir Joseph

I am the mon-arch of the sea, The rul-er of the Queen's Na-
when the breez-es blow, I gen-er-al-ly go be-

Cousin Hebe

vee, Whose praise Great Bri - tain loud - ly chants And we are his
low, And seek the se-clu-sion that a ca - bin grants. And so do his

Chorus

sis-ters and his cous-ins and his aunts, And we are his sis-ters and his
sis-ters and his cous-ins and his aunts, And so do his sis-ters and his

1.

cous-ins and his aunts, His sis-ters and his cous-ins and his aunts. But
cous-ins and his aunts, And

2.

So do his sis-ters and his cous-ins and his aunts, His sis-ters and his cous-ins;

Whom he reck-ons by the doz-ens and his aunts._____

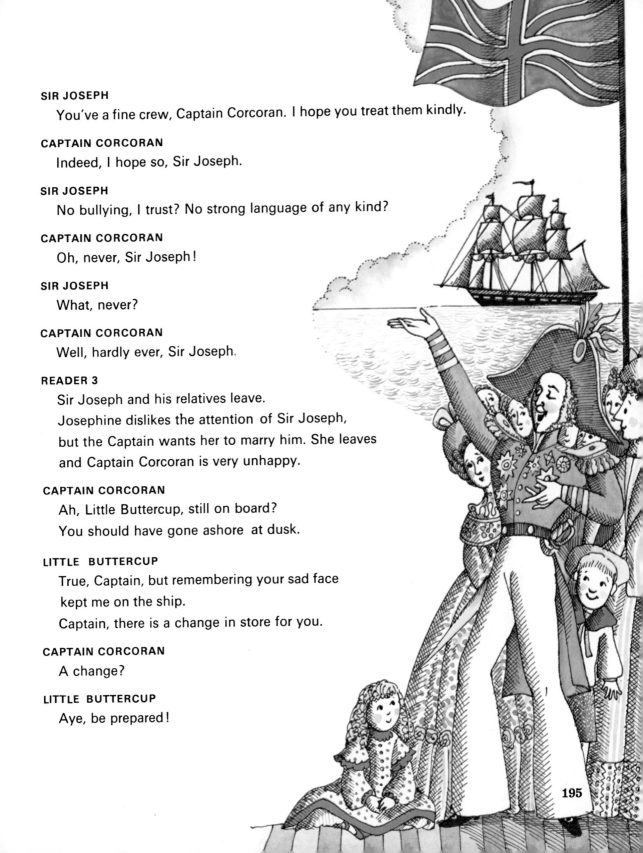

SIR JOSEPH

You've a fine crew, Captain Corcoran. I hope you treat them kindly.

CAPTAIN CORCORAN

Indeed, I hope so, Sir Joseph.

SIR JOSEPH

No bullying, I trust? No strong language of any kind?

CAPTAIN CORCORAN

Oh, never, Sir Joseph!

SIR JOSEPH

What, never?

CAPTAIN CORCORAN

Well, hardly ever, Sir Joseph.

READER 3

Sir Joseph and his relatives leave.
Josephine dislikes the attention of Sir Joseph,
but the Captain wants her to marry him. She leaves
and Captain Corcoran is very unhappy.

CAPTAIN CORCORAN

Ah, Little Buttercup, still on board?
You should have gone ashore at dusk.

LITTLE BUTTERCUP

True, Captain, but remembering your sad face
kept me on the ship.
Captain, there is a change in store for you.

CAPTAIN CORCORAN

A change?

LITTLE BUTTERCUP

Aye, be prepared!

195

Things Are Seldom What They Seem

Buttercup

Things are sel - dom what they seem, Skim milk mas-quer-ades as cream;
Black sheep dwell in ev - 'ry fold; All that glit - ters is not gold;

High - lows pass as pat - ent leath-ers. Jack-daws strut in
Storks turn out to be but logs,___ Bulls are but in-

Captain

pea - cock's feath-ers. Ver - y true, so they do.
flat - ed frogs.___ So they be, fre - quent-ly.

CAPTAIN CORCORAN

I do not understand what new change is coming. Time alone can tell.

READER 1

Little Buttercup leaves as Sir Joseph enters.

SIR JOSEPH

Captain Corcoran, I am much disappointed with your daughter. In fact, I don't think she will do!

CAPTAIN CORCORAN

She won't do, Sir Joseph?

SIR JOSEPH

I'm afraid not. I have courted her without success.

CAPTAIN CORCORAN

Perhaps your exalted rank dazzles her.

SIR JOSEPH

You think it does?

197

CAPTAIN CORCORAN

If your lordship would assure her that love levels all ranks, she might look upon your offer of marriage in its proper light.

SIR JOSEPH

But . . . quiet, here she is. Madam, I am told that you are overcome by my exalted rank. If your hesitation is due to that, it is uncalled for.

JOSEPHINE

Your lordship is of the opinion that married happiness has nothing to do with rank?

SIR JOSEPH

I am of that opinion.

JOSEPHINE

That the high and the lowly may be truly happy together if they love one another?

SIR JOSEPH

Love is a platform upon which all ranks meet.

JOSEPHINE

I thank you, Sir Joseph. I did hesitate, but I will hesitate no longer.

READER 4

Little did Sir Joseph realize how well he had pleaded his rival's cause. Josephine leaves. Sir Joseph and the Captain are most pleased with themselves. Sir Joseph thinks he will marry Josephine, and the Captain is sure that he will soon have a daughter married to a member of the cabinet.

READER 1

All hopes are suddenly dashed by Dick Deadeye, who tells the Captain that Josephine and Ralph plan to run away and be married. The Captain surprises the pair and stops them. Ralph proudly states that he is not just a lowly sailor. He is an Englishman.

He Is an Englishman

Chorus

He is an Eng-lish - man! For _____ he him - self has said ___ it, And it's great-ly to his cred - it, that he is an Eng-lish- man! He re - mains an ___ Eng - - - - lish - man! ___

READER 2

The Captain becomes very angry and uses bad language. Sir Joseph hears him and is very unhappy. The Captain is sent to his cabin. Ralph then tells Sir Joseph that he is proud of his love for Josephine. Sir Joseph is outraged and has Ralph seized and taken to the ship's dungeon. Everything seems hopeless, until Little Buttercup makes a confession.

LITTLE BUTTERCUP

I took care of two babies many years ago. One baby was from a poor family and the other from a wealthy family. I don't know how I did it, but I got those children mixed up! The well-born baby was Ralph. Your Captain was the other!

SIR JOSEPH

Am I to understand that Ralph is really the Captain, and the Captain is Ralph?

LITTLE BUTTERCUP

That is the idea!

SIR JOSEPH

Let them appear before me at once!

READER 2

The Captain and Ralph respond to Sir Joseph's order. They enter together.

SIR JOSEPH

It seems that you were Ralph and Ralph was you.

CAPTAIN CORCORAN

So it seems, your honor.

SIR JOSEPH

I need not tell you that after this change, a marriage with your daughter is out of the question!

CAPTAIN CORCORAN
But your honor, you said that love levels all ranks.

SIR JOSEPH
But not to this extent! Here, Ralph, take her and treat her kindly.

CAPTAIN CORCORAN
Little Buttercup, was this the change you spoke of?

LITTLE BUTTERCUP
Very true, very true.

READER 1
Little Buttercup takes the Captain's hand to comfort him.

SIR JOSEPH

Oh, sad am I! What shall I do? I cannot live alone!

HEBE

Fear nothing. I will take care of you.

SIR JOSEPH

Then tomorrow we will all say our vows. Ralph and Josephine, Captain Corcoran and Little Buttercup, and Hebe and I. Three loving pairs on the same day united.

Finale

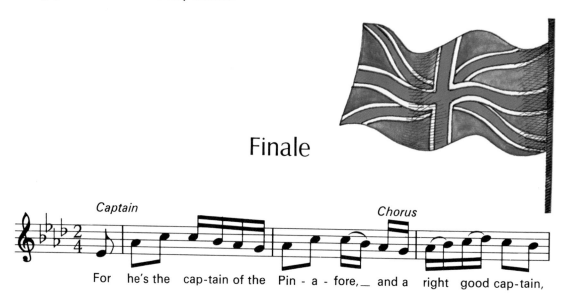

For he's the cap-tain of the Pin - a - fore,__ and a right good cap-tain, too! And though be-fore my fall I was cap-tain of you all, I'm a

mem - ber__ of the crew. And though be-fore his fall He was

cap-tain of us all, He's a mem-ber___ of the crew. I shall

mar-ry with a wife, In my hum-ble rank of life! And you, my own, are___

she. I must wan-der to and fro, But wher-ev-er I may go, I shall

Chorus   *Captain*

nev-er be un-true to thee! What nev-er? No nev-er! What

Chorus   *Captain*   *Chorus and soloists*

nev-er?___ Hard-ly ev-er! Hard-ly ev-er be un-true to

thee, Then give three cheers, and one cheer more, For the form-er cap-tain of the

Continued on next page   **203**

Pin - a - fore. Then give three cheers, and one cheer more, For the

cap-tain of the Pin - a - fore.

Buttercup

For he loves lit - tle

But - ter - cup, dear lit - tle But - ter - cup, Though I could nev - er tell

why; _____ But still he loves But - ter - cup, poor lit - tle But - ter - cup,

Sir Joseph

Sweet lit - tle But - ter - cup, aye! I'm the mon-arch of the sea, And

when I've mar - ried thee, I'll be true to the de - vo - tion that my

Cousin Hebe

love im-plants, Then good-bye to your sis-ters, and your cous-ins, and your aunts, Es-

204

pe - cial - ly your cous - ins, Whom you reck-on up by doz - ens then good-

bye to your sis - ters, and your cous - ins and your aunts. Es -

pe - cial - ly your cous-ins whom you reck-on up by doz - ens and your

aunts! _____ For he is an Eng - lish - man! _____ For _____

he him - self has said ___ it, And it's great - ly to his

cred - it That he is an Eng - lish - man! That he

is ___ an ___ Eng - - - - - - lish - man!

The perspectives of music

Music helps people celebrate. Music helps people express their feelings about their country, their friends, and important events in life. While the other sections of this book are concerned with the nature of music itself, this section shows how important music has been through the ages and how important it is today.

"Across the Continent" is a lithograph which celebrates an important event in 19th century America—establishing a railroad across the country from New York to San Francisco. It is an example of the kinds of events that are of interest to artists. These also include themes such as religion, politics, and celebrations.

People, music, and homeland

Although it is exciting to travel, the traveler is usually glad to return home. It is always good to see familiar people and things.

Although people change the location of their homes much more frequently today than in former times, they often feel a close relationship to their place of birth. Poetry, stories, music, and art often reflect people's feelings for their homeland.

I Ride an Old Paint

Cowboy Song

1. I ride an old Paint, I lead an old Dan,
2. Oh, when I die, take my sad - dle from the wall,

I'm goin' to Mon - tan - a to throw the hou - li - han,
And put it on my pon-y, lead him out of his stall.

They feed in the cou - lees, they wa - ter in the draw,
Tie my bones to his back, turn our fac - es to the west,

Their tails are all mat - ted, their backs are all raw.
And we'll ride the prai - rie that we love the best.

Refrain

Ride a - round lit - tle do - gies, Ride a - round them slow,

For they're fier - y and snuf - fy and a rar - in' to go.

Home on the Range

Cowboy Song
Arranged by M. Rinehart

Voices (or Bells)

Ah _____

1. O give me a home where the buf - fa - lo roam, Where the
2. The air is so pure and the zeph - yrs so free, And the
3. How of - ten at night when the heav - ens are bright, With the

deer and the an - te - lope play, _____ Where
breez - es so balm - y and light, _____ That I
light from the glit - ter - ing stars, _____ Have I

Ah _____

sel - dom is heard a dis - cour - ag - ing word, And the
would not ex - change my __ home on the range For __
stood there a - mazed and __ asked as I gazed, If their

skies   are   not   cloud - y   all   day._____
all   of   the   cit - ies   so   bright._____
glo -   ry ex - ceeds   that   of   ours._____

Home,____ home on the range, ____   Where the   deer

Home,   home on the range,____ where the deer and the an - te -lope

play,_____   Ah _____

play, _____ Where sel - dom is heard a dis - cour - ag -ing word, And the

skies   are   not   cloud - y   all   day._____

In this song an Indian youth remembers the wild life and natural beauty of his land. Find the words of the song that seem to express a yearning for the homeland. Sing the song at different tempos to find the speed that best expresses this yearning. Try various dynamics as well. You can accompany the song with this drum pattern.

This watercolor was painted by Alfred Jacob Miller in 1837. The theme of this picture is similar to that of the song "Land of the Silver Birch." This picture gives you the impression of looking out over a vast area. Creating the Illusion of depth in a landscape is called "atmospheric perspective." What devices did Miller use to create this illusion?

Paint your own landscape. Make some objects seem near and others far away.

Land of the Silver Birch

Canadian Folk Song

1. Land of the sil - ver birch, home of the bea - ver,
2. Down in the for - est, deep in the low - lands,
3. High on a rock - y ledge, I'll build a wig - wam,

Where still the might - y moose wan - ders at will,
My heart cries out for thee, hills of the north.
Close by the wa - ter's edge, si - lent and still.

Blue lake and rock - y shore, I will re - turn once more.

Boom de de boom boom, Boom de de boom boom, Boom de de boom boom,

Boom.

Waterloo Music Company Limited for "Land of the Silver Birch" from
FOLK SONGS OF CANADA by Edith Fowke & Richard Johnston,
published by Waterloo Music Company Limited.

Many people leave their homes at some time in their lives and travel to other lands. When Swiss people are away from their homeland, they long for the tall mountains and the green valleys of the Swiss countryside.

Beyond the Mountain

Swiss Folk Song
English text by
Marilyn Keith and Alan Bergman
Arranged by C. A. R.

1. There lies a world be-yond the moun-tains, there lies a
2. My fath-er lived be-neath the moun-tains, as did his
3. And so, fare-well, O friend-ly moun-tains. The time has

world for me to see. And I must go be-yond the
fath-er long a-go. And I was born be-neath the
come for me to roam. And e'er I go be-yond the

moun-tains and leave the home so dear to me.
moun-tains. They are the on-ly home I know.
moun-tains, I know my heart will long for home.

Refrain (Descant)

La la la la la la la la, la la la la la la la

Refrain (Melody)

La la la la la la la la la, la la la la la la la

214

la la, And I must go be - yond the moun - tains And___

la la, And I must go be - yond the moun - tains And___

leave the home so dear to me.

leave the home so dear to me.

In this photograph of the Swiss Alps there are rich contrasts between quiet meadows and dramatic mountain peaks. There is a great range of color—green, gray, blue, violet, and earth colors. There are textures ranging from the smoothness of grassy meadows to the ruggedness of rocks.

The beauty of Norway is described in this Norwegian folk song. The brilliant snow-capped mountains make a striking contrast with the deep blue waters of the fjords and the green summer meadows.

A feeling of longing for the homeland is expressed through the music as well as through the words.

I Remember This Land

Norwegian Folk Song
English text by Carroll Rinehart

1. I re-mem-ber this land where the tall moun-tains stand, where the
2. I re-mem-ber with joy how I roamed as a boy, how I

sun shines so bright at____ sum - mer's mid - night. O it's
shout - ed and sang; how my ech - oes all rang. It is

there I long to go, where the fjords are laced with snow; All its
there I lived and played; where such beau - ty is dis - played; And from

beau - ty is a - glow!
there have I now strayed.
I re -

I re-mem - ber, re-mem - ber this land.

Melody

mem - ber so well; I re-mem - ber this land.

This is a photograph of a portion of a work by Norway's greatest sculptor, Gustav Vigeland. It is a sculpture of three boys gazing into the sky, and it is carved out of granite. Notice that the human form has been simplified but still remains true to nature. How are contrasts of dark and light created?

Czechoslovakia has been captured many times by larger, more powerful countries. In spite of this, the Czechs have maintained an independent spirit. They remain proud of their beautiful land.

Over the Meadow

Czech Folk Song
English text by A. D. Zanzig

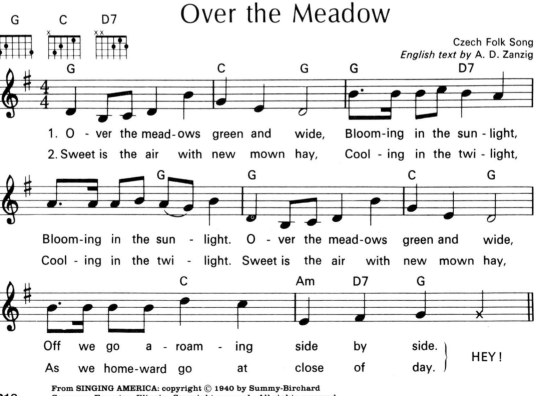

1. O - ver the mead-ows green and wide, Bloom-ing in the sun - light,
2. Sweet is the air with new mown hay, Cool - ing in the twi - light,

Bloom-ing in the sun - light. O - ver the mead-ows green and wide,
Cool - ing in the twi - light. Sweet is the air with new mown hay,

Off we go a - roam - ing side by side. ⎫ HEY!
As we home-ward go at close of day. ⎭

219

Westering Home

Words by Hugh S. Roberton

West-er-ing home, and a song in the air, Light in the eye, and it's

good-bye to care; Laugh-ter o' love and a wel-com-ing there,

Isle of my heart, my own one!

Tell me o' lands o' the O -ri -ent gay! Sing o' the rich -es and

joys o' Ca-thay! Eh, but it's grand to be wa -kin' ilk* day, To

find your -self near - er to Is - la. (And it's)

*ilk—each

My Heart's in the Highlands

My heart's in the Highlands, my heart is not here;
My heart's in the Highlands a-chasing the deer;
A-hunting the wild deer and chasing the roe;
My heart's in the Highlands wherever I go.

Robert Burns

Have you ever passed through a familiar place and tried to remember what happened when you were there before? In this Japanese folk song, a person remembers what happened when he walked down a certain road. How do you think he felt about this familiar place? How would he sing the song?

Oh, I Remember

Japanese Folk Song
English text by Katherine Rohrbaugh

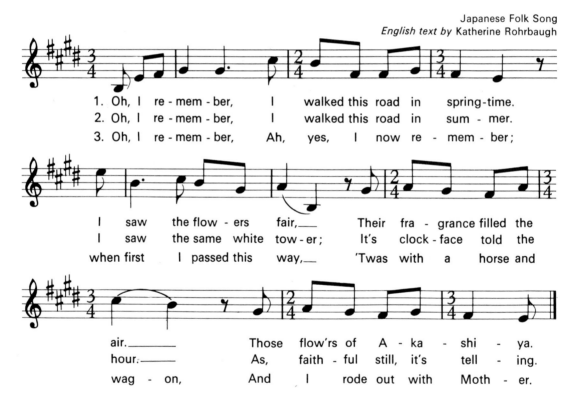

1. Oh, I re-mem-ber, I walked this road in spring-time.
2. Oh, I re-mem-ber, I walked this road in sum-mer.
3. Oh, I re-mem-ber, Ah, yes, I now re-mem-ber;

I saw the flow-ers fair,___ Their fra-grance filled the
I saw the same white tow-er; It's clock-face told the
when first I passed this way,___ 'Twas with a horse and

air.___ Those flow'rs of A-ka-shi-ya.
hour.___ As, faith-ful still, it's tell-ing.
wag-on, And I rode out with Moth-er.

Look at the meter signature. What happens to the meter in this song? How does this affect the mood of the song?

Make up an accompaniment for the song with the E, F♯, G♯, B, and C♯ bells.

After a day of work, the workers paddle their boats home-ward. They sing as they dip the oars, "Sun ah go down slow, slow." Before the night comes, the workers want some time to enjoy their family and home.

Sun Ah Go Down

Fairly slow

Guiana Folk Song

Wool-lah, wool-lah, wool-lay, wool-lay, Sun ah go down slow, slow.

Wool-lah, wool-lah, wool-lay, wool-lay, Sun ah go down slow,

Freely

slow. A - way, me man-nie doh toh tay, A -

way me man-nie doh toh tay, A - way me man-nie

doh toh tay, Sun ah go down slow, slow.

COMPOSE A SONG ABOUT YOUR HOMELAND

1. Choose a subject for your song. Is there a place where you once lived that you would like to visit? Perhaps you spent a summer in a place you remember with pleasure. Imagine that you have traveled far from your present home and that you are thinking of coming back.

2. Decide what you want to tell about in your song. Perhaps it is a place where you meet your friends after school and you want to tell about those meetings; perhaps you would like to tell about a quiet spot where you like to go and think.

3. Write some words for your song; they need not rhyme. Include the ideas you have chosen. Choose a melody you already know, or compose one. The melody should express the mood you feel. Perform the song for your classmates.

National Gallery of Art, Washington, D.C.

George Innes painted this romantic landscape in 1855. "The Lackawanna Valley" is painted as though seen through the eyes of the child in the foreground—everything seems perfect.

Innes was a great admirer of nature and tried to capture its poetry while telling us about the scene he was painting. He wanted people to respond emotionally to his works.

Nationalism and romanticism in music

The feeling of national pride in the European nations became very strong during the 1800's. Composers, artists, and authors became interested in the folk legends of their homelands. National songs, folk dances, and folk heroes became important material for their works.

Nationalism

The strong sense of national identity in music, art, and literature is referred to as **nationalism.**

Jan Sibelius was a composer who was greatly influenced by the nationalistic movement during the late nineteenth century. Finland, Sibelius' homeland, is a beautiful country with many lakes and forests.

Find Finland on a map of Europe. You will see that it is very far north. Winters in Finland are long and dark, and life is very rugged. Because of Finland's location between Russia and Sweden, it has often served as a battleground for it's more powerful neighbors. The Finns, however, have remained proud, strong, and independent people.

LISTENING *Finlandia*
Jan Sibelius

Sibelius' love for his country is expressed in his music. His best-known work is *Finlandia,* a composition for orchestra. The work begins with a powerful theme played by the brass instruments.

The music builds in excitement until a long chord signals the entrance of the second theme, which is a quiet, hymnlike melody. Which instruments introduce this theme?

In the third section of the work, some of the music from the first section is combined with the hymn-like melody. This section builds to a powerful climax.

The second theme from *Finlandia* is also a song. Many different words have been set to this music. The powerful melody is meaningful to people throughout the world.

Song of Peace

Music by Jan Sibelius
Words by Leland Isaac

This is my hope— a hope that all the na - tions____

____ Will live in peace with love for all man - kind.____

____ For when the earth is filled with strife and dark - ness____

____ All hope is gone and joy is left be - hind.

____ So let there be true har - mon - y and kind - ness____

____ That all the world a way to peace may find.____

Music will probably always be important in helping people feel part of a group. Singing the school song is a way of expressing group identity. What songs do you know that are used to create a group feeling?

In the 1950's and 1960's, the song "We Shall Overcome" was sung by people who worked in the Civil Rights Movement. What words in the text of the song made it effective in bringing the people together? Why do you suppose the melody became so popular?

We Shall Overcome

American Freedom Song

1. We shall o - ver - come,_____ We shall o - ver - come,_____
2. We'll walk hand in hand,_____ We'll walk hand in hand,_____

We shall o - ver - come some day; _____ Oh!___
We'll walk hand in hand some day; _____ Oh!___

deep in my heart I do be - lieve,
deep in my heart I do be - lieve,

We shall o - ver - come some day. _____
We'll walk hand in hand some day. _____

3. We are not afraid . . . *etc.*
   We are not afraid today.

4. We shall brothers be . . . *etc.*
   We shall brothers be some day.

5. Truth shall make us free . . . *etc.*
   Truth shall make us free some day.

229

"The Battle and Defeat of Napoleon" from
HÁRY JÁNOS SUITE
Zoltán Kodály

Zoltán Kodály was a Hungarian composer who collected the folk music of his country. Kodály's interest in the folklore of his country is expressed in his comic opera, *Háry János*. Later, some of the music from this opera was made into an orchestral suite. The opera tells the story of Háry János, a folk hero who had fantastic adventures. János is an elderly peasant with great imagination. He likes to sit in the village inn and tell his friends of his adventures from the past.

János tells the story of Marie Louise, wife of Napoleon, who once stopped in the village on her way to Vienna. She happened to see János, then a young man, and immediately fell in love with him.

Napoleon, hearing of this, arrived with his army. But the bold János went to meet the enemy. János had no trouble defeating Napoleon's army.

TROMBONE

Finally there was no one left but Napoleon. Snare drums and brass instruments announce the arrival of Napoleon.

DRUMS AND BRASS

SAXOPHONE

Napoleon retreated, begging for mercy as he went. Kodály uses the somber tones of the saxophone to describe the defeated emperor.

LISTENING *"The Ride of the Valkyries" from THE VALKYRIES*
Richard Wagner

Richard Wagner, a German composer, based many of his operas on German legends. "The Ride of the Valkyries" is from the opera *The Valkyries*. The Valkyries are the nine daughters of Wotan, king of the gods. These maidens ride winged horses through the sky. The music you will hear represents their ride to a meeting at a rocky mountain top.

How does this theme suggest galloping horses?

BRASS

What instruments did the composer use to build a climax?
What happens near the end of the piece?

The Romantic Age

The nineteenth century is often referred to as the Romantic Age. During this time, composers, artists, and writers became very interested in expressing deep, personal feelings in their works. The compositions of the romantic composers—Brahms, Schumann, Schubert, Chopin, Tchaikovsky, Wagner, Grieg, and many others—are popular today.

During the Romantic Age, a new type of musical work became popular. These works were often short, and each piece expressed one mood.

LISTENING   *Waltz in C♯ Minor, Op. 64, No. 2*
Prelude in G Minor, Op. 28, No. 22
Etude in G♭, Op. 25, No. 9
Frédéric Chopin

What mood does each of these three pieces express? Which of the following phrases best describe the music of Chopin?

few dynamic contrasts
many dynamic contrasts

short, fragmented melodies
long, sustained melodies

little harmonic interest
rich harmonies

Often the words of a song are a poem. One type of song that expresses the mood or idea of a poem is the **art song.** The piano accompaniment can be a very important part of the art song and often contributes to the overall mood. Many art songs were written during the Romantic Age.

The Linden Tree (excerpt)

(Der Lindenbaum)

Music by Franz Schubert
Words by W. Müller

Be-side   the old stone foun-tain,   There stands a Lin - den tree;
Am Brun - nen vor dem Tor - re,   da steht ein Lin - den - baum;

Be - neath it's spread-ing branch-es   Glad dreams have come to me.
ich traümt' in sei - nem Schat - ten   so man - chen sü - ssen Traum.

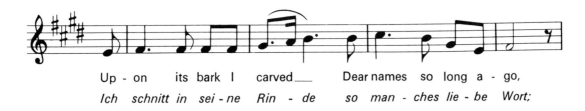

Up - on   its bark I   carved___ Dear names so long a - go,
Ich schnitt in sei - ne Rin - de   so man - ches lie - be Wort;

I sought its peace in glad - ness,   I sought_ its peace in woe.
es zog in Freud'und Lei - de   zu ihm___ mich im - mer fort.

| LISTENING | *Der Lindenbaum*
Franz Schubert

Listen to the recording of Schubert's "Der Lindenbaum."
What happens to the music at the beginning of the second
verse? How does this reflect the change of mood in the text?

233

"View of Toledo" was painted at the beginning of the 17th century by El Greco. It is a very dramatic painting. It appeals strongly to our emotions through the contrast of light and dark.

Paint a dramatic picture. Work with line and color to create a strong emotional effect.

Music for the seasons

A Vagabond Song

There is something in the autumn that is native to my blood—
Touch of manner, hint of mood;
And my heart is like a rhyme,
With the yellow and the purple and the crimson keeping time.

The scarlet of the maples can shake me like a cry
Of bugles going by.
And my lonely spirit thrills
To see the frosty asters like smoke upon the hills.

There is something in October sets the gypsy blood astir;
We must rise and follow her,
When from every hill of flame
She calls and calls each vagabond by name.

Bliss Carman

The word "Halloween" is a shortened form of "All Hallow's Eve." The night of October 31 is the time when devils and witches supposedly have an all-night celebration before All Saints Day, November 1.

Witches' Brew

Music by Edith Savage
Words by Carroll Rinehart

Stir, stir the witch-es' brew! Stir, stir, the whole night through!

Stoke the fire,___ keep it hot,___ All must stir the witch-es' pot!___

Dou-ble, dou-ble, toil and trou-ble, Fire___ burn and caul-dron bub-ble!

What in the brew will the witch-es throw As round the pot their fa-ces glow?___

Toes of frogs and old black bats, Hairs of dogs and old dead cats.

Dou-ble, dou-ble, toil and trou-ble, Fire___ burn and caul-dron bub-ble.

Thanksgiving celebrations usually take place after the summer crops are harvested. In many parts of the world, harvested straw and grain are used to make special decorations for the harvest celebrations.

The words and melody of "Harvesters" express the enthusiasm and joy that harvest time brings.

Harvesters

Alsatian Folk Song
Words by Katherine Rohrbaugh

Be - fore the morn - ing star has set, while fields with dew - drops still are wet, we rise from sleep__ and take__ our way To reap the grain__ this har - vest day. Where do you go, oh, star, so bright, when day's__ warm sun - shine dims your light?

The Pilgrims' thanksgiving is the subject of this picture, which was once an illustration for a magazine article. By looking at the painting, one can learn about the Pilgrims' housing and about the style of clothing worn by both Pilgrims and Indians. The purpose of an illustration is usually to inform, not to arouse deep feelings. Illustrations are not always significant works of art.

"We Gather Together" is a folk tune from the Netherlands. The words of the song are those of a prayer and a plea for freedom. In America this song has become a traditional Thanksgiving hymn.

We Gather Together

Netherland Folk Song
Translation by T. Baker

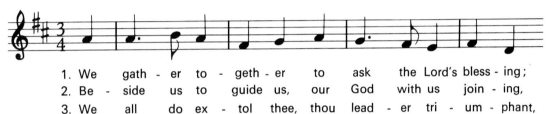

1. We gath - er to - geth - er to ask the Lord's bless - ing;
2. Be - side us to guide us, our God with us join - ing,
3. We all do ex - tol thee, thou lead - er tri - um - phant,

He chas - tens and has - tens his will to make known;
Or - dain - ing, main - tain - ing his king - dom di - vine;
And pray that thou still our de - fend - er will be.

The wick - ed op - press - ing now cease____ from dis - tress - ing,
So from the be - gin - ning the fight____ we were win - ning;
Let thy con - gre - ga - tion es - cape____ trib - u - la - tion;

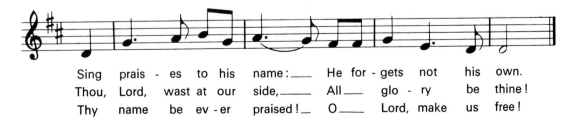

Sing prais - es to his name:____ He for - gets not his own.
Thou, Lord, wast at our side,____ All____ glo - ry be thine!
Thy name be ev - er praised!__ O____ Lord, make us free!

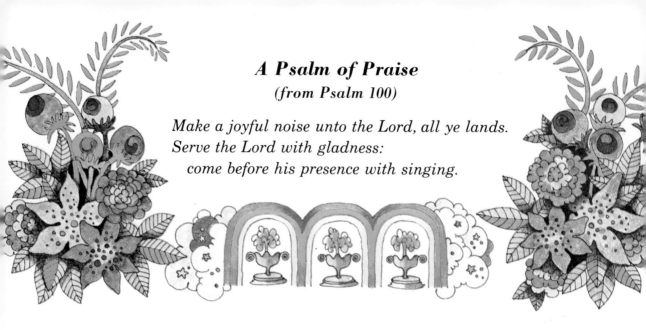

A Psalm of Praise
(from Psalm 100)

Make a joyful noise unto the Lord, all ye lands.
Serve the Lord with gladness:
*   come before his presence with singing.*

Joyful, Joyful, We Adore Thee

Music arranged from Ludwig van Beethoven
Words by Henry van Dyke

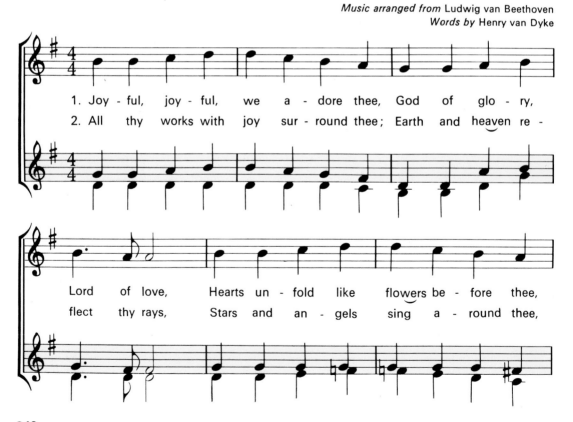

1. Joy - ful, joy - ful, we a - dore thee, God of glo - ry,
2. All thy works with joy sur - round thee; Earth and heaven re -

Lord of love, Hearts un - fold like flowers be - fore thee,
flect thy rays, Stars and an - gels sing a - round thee,

LISTENING *Symphony No. 9, Movement 4, excerpt*
Ludwig van Beethoven

The melody of "Joyful, Joyful, We Adore Thee" is taken from the last movement of Beethoven's *Symphony No. 9.* Listen for places where there is a sudden change of mood.

Winter

"Wassailing" is a traditional English custom practiced at Christmas time. Groups of people go from house to house singing carols. The carolers are often invited in to share holiday food and drink.

Wassail Song

Old English Carol

1. 𝄾 Here we come a - was - sail - ing a - mong the leaves so
2. We are not dai - ly beg - gars that beg from door to
3. Good mas - ter and mis - tress, as you sit by the
4. God bless the mas - ter of this house, like - wise the mis - tress

green; _____ 𝄾 Here we come a - wan - d'ring, so
door; _____ But we are neigh - bors' chil - dren whom
fire; _____ Pray think of us poor chil - dren who
too, _____ And all the lit - tle chil - dren that

fair _____ to be seen.
you have seen be - fore.
wan - der in the mire.
round the ta - ble go.

Love and joy come to you, And to

you glad Christ-mas too; And God bless you and send___ you a

hap - py New Year, And God send you a hap - py New Year.

"God Rest You Merry, Gentlemen" is a traditional caroling song which tells the Christmas Story.

God Rest You Merry, Gentlemen

Traditional English Carol

1. God rest you mer - ry, gen - tle - men, Let noth - ing you dis - may,
2. In Beth - le - hem, in Jew - ry, This bless - ed Babe was born,
3. Now to the Lord sing prais - es, All you with - in this place,

Re - mem - ber Christ our Sav - iour Was born on Christ - mas Day;
And laid with - in a man - ger, Up - on this bless - ed morn;
And with true love and broth - er - hood Each oth - er now em - brace;

To save us all from Sa - tan's pow'r When we were gone a - stray.
The which his moth - er Ma - ry, Did noth - ing take in scorn.
This hol - y tide of Christ - mas All oth - ers doth de - face.

O ___ ti - dings of com - fort and joy, com - fort and joy,

O ___ ti - dings of com - fort and joy.

England's Carol
Modern Jazz Quartet

"England's Carol" is an improvisation on "God Rest You Merry, Gentlemen." An improvisation is music that is created and performed at the same time. This improvisation is done by the Modern Jazz Quartet.

The members of the quartet play piano, vibraphone, string bass, and percussion. The Modern Jazz Quartet plays with a symphony orchestra on the recording.

Sometimes the melody of the carol is easy to recognize. Sometimes only small parts of the melody are heard. At other times, the improvisation departs from the melody completely.

CAREERS

Creativity and musical skill are two qualities necessary for **jazz musicians,** as they often improvise during performances. Piano, string bass, drums, trombone, trumpet, saxophone, clarinet, and guitar are the most common instruments in jazz groups.

© James Theologos/MONKMEYER PRESS PHOTO SERVICE

LISTENING *Serenade of Carols, Movement 4*
Morton Gould

"Serenade of Carols," for small orchestra, is in four movements. In the last movement, the composer uses four carols: "Irish Carol," "God Rest You Merry, Gentlemen," "Wassail Song," and "My Dancing Day."

How is the melody of "God Rest You Merry, Gentlemen" used in this composition? In what ways is this use different from that in "England's Carol"?

The castles of old England were centers of holiday festivities. The great halls were decorated, and a huge Yule log was brought in for the fire. The burning of the Yule log was thought to bring good luck. As long as the Yule log burned, no work was done. As you might imagine, the largest and best log was chosen for the holidays.

Deck the Halls

Welsh Carol
Arranged by Carroll A. Rinehart

Descant

1. Deck the halls with hol - ly,
2. See the Yule be - fore us,
3. Fast the old year pass - es,
Fa la la la la, la la la la.

Melody

1. Deck the halls with boughs of hol - ly,
2. See the blaz - ing Yule be - fore us,
3. Fast a - way the old year pass - es,
Fa la la la la, la la la la.

'Tis the sea - son jol - ly,
Strike the harp and cho - rus,
Hail the new, ye lass - es,
Fa la la la la, la la la la.

'Tis the sea - son to be jol - ly,
Strike the harp and join the cho - rus,
Hail the new, ye lads and lass - es,
Fa la la la la, la la la la.

| C7 | F | Dm | G7 | C | G7 | C |

Fa la, Fa la, Fa la la, la la la, la la la.

Don we now our gay ap-par - rel,
Fol - low me in mer - ry meas-ure, } Fa la la, la la la, la la la.
Sing we joy-ous all to-geth - er,

Troll the Yule-tide car - ol,
While I tell of treas-ure, } Fa la la la la, la la la la.
Heed - less of the weath-er,

Troll the an - cient Yule-tide car - ol,
While I tell of Yule-tide treas-ure, } Fa la la la la, la la la la.
Heed - less of the wind and weath-er,

Imitation is used in this arrangement of "Deck the Halls."
Which parts of the descant are an imitation of the melody?

The carol "Shepherd, Shake off Your Drowsy Sleep" comes from a part of France located near Switzerland. The countryside there is hilly and suitable for grazing sheep. Perhaps this is why the people of that area chose the shepherds of Bethlehem as subjects for this lively carol.

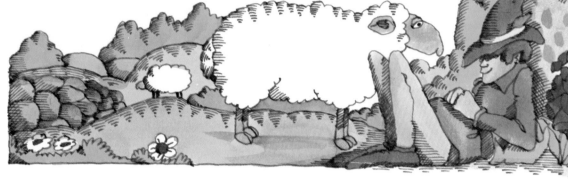

Shepherd, Shake off Your Drowsy Sleep

Besançon Carol
Arranged by Carroll A. Rinehart

Shep-herd, shake off your drow-sy sleep, Rise and leave your sil - ly
Ber - ger, se - coue ton som-meil pro-fond! Leve-toi et laisse tes mou-tons jou-

sheep; An - gels from Heav'n a - round are sing - ing, Ti - dings
er; An - ges du Ciel chan-tant très for - te Ap - por-tez-

Refrain

of___ great joy__ are bring - ing. Shep-herd, the cho - rus come and
nous__ la grande nou - vel - le. Ber - ger, en choeur chan-tez No-

swell! Sing No - el, O sing____ No - el.
el, O, chan - tez No - el, ____ No - el.

2. See how the flowers all burst anew
Thinking snow is summer dew;
See how the stars afresh are glowing
All their brightest beams bestowing.
Refrain

2. *Vois comme les fleurs s'ouvrent de nouveau,*
Vois que la neige est rosée d'été,
Vois les étoiles brillent de nouveau
Jetant leurs rayons les plus lumineaux
Refrain

3. Shepherd, then up and quick away!
Seek the babe ere break of day.
He is the hope of every nation,
All in Him shall find salvation.
Refrain

3. *Berger, levez-vous, hâtez-vous!*
Allez chercher l'Enfant avant le jour
Il est l'espoir de chaque nation,
Tous en Lui trouveront la Rédemption
Refrain

249

Come, All Ye Shepherds

Czech Carol *Arranged by* Carroll A. Rinehart

1. Come, all ye shep-herds and hark to our
2. Come, all ye shep-herds a - rise, leave your

1. Come, ye shep - herds, hark, our
2. Come, ye shep - herds, leave your

song! Come, all ye shep-herds, Christ Je-sus is
sheep! Come to the sta - ble, Lord Je-sus to

song! Come, ye shep - herds, Je - sus is
sheep! To the sta - ble, Je - sus to

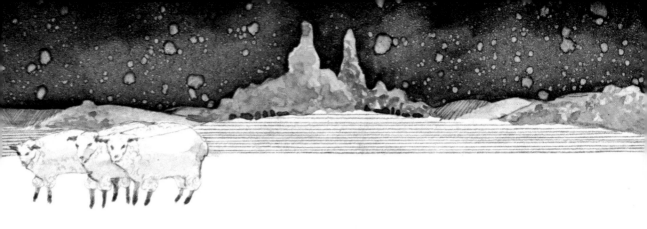

born !
seek !

Lo ! un - to us this day there is giv - en
Lo, in a man - ger lies Christ a - noint-ed,

born !
seek !
}
Glo - ry, Glo - ry,

Our Lord, Christ Je - sus, sent down from Heav - en !
Whom, as our Sav-ior, God has ap - point-ed,
}
Glo - ry to God on high.

Glo - ry, Glo - ry, Glo - ry on high !

251

The song "In Bethlehem" tells the Christmas story that the animals in the stable might have told.

Find the melodic sequence in the last half of "In Bethlehem." What happens to the pitch of the pattern each time it is repeated?

In Bethlehem

Words and music
by Malvina Reynolds
Arranged by Carroll A. Rinehart

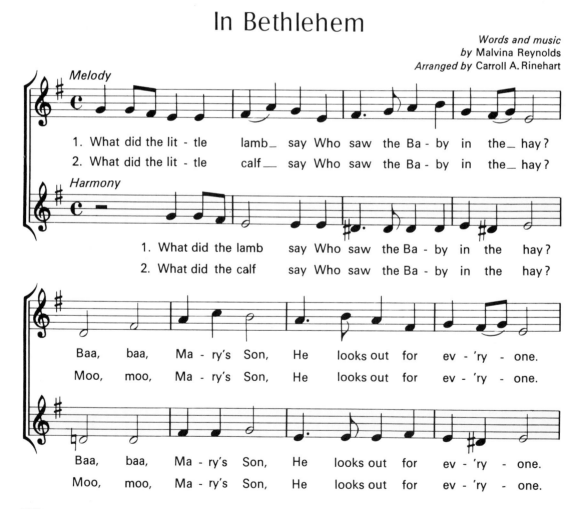

Melody

1. What did the lit - tle lamb_ say Who saw the Ba - by in the_ hay?
2. What did the lit - tle calf_ say Who saw the Ba - by in the_ hay?

Harmony

1. What did the lamb say Who saw the Ba - by in the hay?
2. What did the calf say Who saw the Ba - by in the hay?

Baa, baa, Ma - ry's Son, He looks out for ev - 'ry - one.
Moo, moo, Ma - ry's Son, He looks out for ev - 'ry - one.

Baa, baa, Ma - ry's Son, He looks out for ev - 'ry - one.
Moo, moo, Ma - ry's Son, He looks out for ev - 'ry - one.

All the sheep are in the fold, No more lamb-ies lost and cold,
All the kine are housed and fed, But no place for Jes - us' head,

All the sheep are in the fold, No more lamb-ies lost and cold,
All the kine are housed and fed, But no place for Jes - us' head,

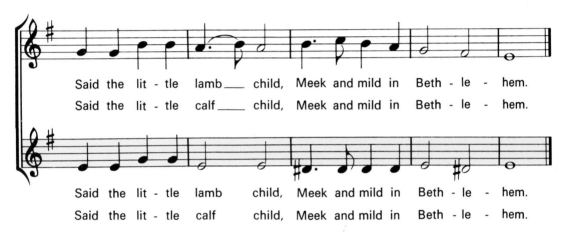

Said the lit - tle lamb___ child, Meek and mild in Beth - le - hem.
Said the lit - tle calf___ child, Meek and mild in Beth - le - hem.

Said the lit - tle lamb child, Meek and mild in Beth - le - hem.
Said the lit - tle calf child, Meek and mild in Beth - le - hem.

3. What did the little chick say
   Who saw the Baby in the hay?
   Tweet, Tweet, Mary's Son,
   He looks out for ev'ryone.
   No more wee ones pushed aside,
   Put to scorn at Christmastide,
   Said the little chick child,
   Meek and mild, in Bethlehem.

4. What did the little foal say
   Who saw the Baby in the hay?
   Nay, Nay, Mary's Son,
   He looks out for ev'ryone
   Time for work and time to feast,
   Time for joy for man and beast,
   Said the little foal child,
   Meek and mild, in Bethlehem.

"A Child Was Born in Bethlehem" has been sung in Europe for many centuries. Johann Sebastian Bach used the same melody in an organ composition.

A Child Was Born in Bethlehem

Ancient Hymn
Text adapted by Carroll A. Rinehart
from translation by Erling Tomasson

Puer Natus in Bethlehem
Arranged for organ by Johann Sebastian Bach

In Bach's organ composition "Puer Natus in Bethlehem," the feeling of the melody changes. Listen to the different harmonies and the motion of the accompaniment.

"Rock of Ages" is a well-known Hanukah song. This song is about the desire of all men for freedom to live and worship as they wish.

Rock of Ages

Old Jewish Melody
Words by G. Gottheil

1. Rock of a - ges, let our song Praise Thy sav - ing— pow - er;
2. Chil - dren of the mar - tyr race, Wheth - er free or— fet - tered,

Thou, a - midst the rag - ing foes, Wast our shel - t'ring tow - er.
Wake the ech - oes of the songs, Where ye may be— scat - tered.

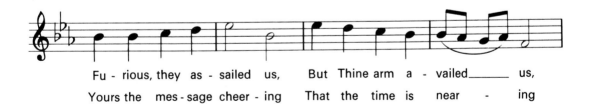

Fu - rious, they as - sailed us, But Thine arm a - vailed_____ us,
Yours the mes - sage cheer - ing That the time is near - ing

And Thy word broke their sword When our own strength failed— us.
Which will see all men free, Ty - rants dis - ap - pear - ing.

255

"In Winter" is a rhythm composition that you can use for experiments in sound. First chant the words several times in rhythm. As you will notice, the rhythm of the notes does not always follow the rhythm of the words, so watch out! When you are familiar with the composition, try some of the ideas on the next page.

In Winter

Heidi Friedlander

A sound-slide show

Sweet Land of Liberty

1. Plan a presentation about something in your community or country that is important to you.

2. Photograph scenes that tell your story in pictures. You might have your friends be actors to help tell your story. Or, you might draw pictures to illustrate your story.

3. Choose music that conveys the mood of your story.

4. Arrange the picture slides or art work in the order you desire. Write your script to accompany the pictures. Then record the narrative. (You might use some percussion sound to tell when to move to the next picture.)

5. Present your work. Invite others to be film critics. Have them describe the ways in which the choice of music, slides or art, and the narration helped to tell your main idea.

Because of the birthdays of George Washington and Abraham Lincoln, February is a traditional time for honoring our country. Singing songs that tell of America's natural beauty and the love of freedom is an important part of patriotic celebrations.

Columbia, the Gem of the Ocean

Attributed to Thomas à Becket

Oh, Co-lum - bia, the gem of the o-cean,

The home of the brave __ and the free, _____

The shrine of each pa - triot's de - vo - tion,

A world __ of - fers hom - age to thee;

Thy___ man - dates make he - roes as - sem - ble,

When___ Lib - er - ty's form stands in view;

Thy___ ban - ners make tyr - an - ny trem - ble

When___ borne___ by the red, white, and blue.

Refrain

When___ borne by the red, white, and blue,

When___ borne by the red, white, and blue,

Thy___ ban - ners make tyr - an - ny trem - ble

When___ borne___ by the red, white, and blue.

The words to our national anthem were written in 1814 when England and the United States were at war. Francis Scott Key and another American had boarded a British warship to try to free an American prisoner. They were held there overnight until the British could carry out their plans to destroy Fort McHenry. Fort McHenry was protecting Baltimore, Maryland, and Key knew that the fort was poorly armed. All night Key watched the shore closely to see what was happening. Shortly after dawn the mist cleared, and Key saw the American flag. Key was overjoyed; he grabbed an envelope and quickly wrote some poetry on it.

When Key returned to Baltimore, he finished the poem. Someone suggested that the poem be sung to the old English tune "To Anacreon in Heaven." A few days later the song was performed for the first time.

The Star-Spangled Banner

Music attributed to J. S. Smith
Words by Francis Scott Key

1. Oh,___ say! can you see, by the dawn's ear - ly light,
2. On the shore, dim - ly seen thro' the mists of the deep,
3. Oh,___ thus be it ev-er when___ free men shall stand

What so proud - ly we hailed at the twi - light's last gleam-ing?
Where the foe's haugh-ty host in dread si - lence re - pos - es,
Be - tween their loved homes and the war's des - o - la - tion!

Whose broad stripes and bright stars, through the per - il - ous fight,
What is that which the breeze, o'er the tow - er - ing steep,
Blest with vic - t'ry and peace, may the heav'n res - cued land

O'er the ram - parts we watched were so gal - lant - ly stream-ing?
As it fit - ful - ly blows, half con - ceals, half dis - clos - es?
Praise the Pow'r that hath made and pre - served us a na - tion.

And the rock - ets' red glare, the bombs burst - ing in air,
Now it catch - es the gleam of the morn - ing's first beam,
Then_ con - quer we must, for our cause it is just,

Gave proof through the night that our flag was still there.
In full glo - ry re - flect-ed now_ shines on the stream;
And this be our mot-to "In_ God is our trust."

Oh, say, does that_ Star - Span - gled Ban - ner_ yet_ wave_
'Tis the Star - Span - gled_ Ban - ner, oh, long may_ it_ wave_
And the Star - Span - gled_ Ban - ner, in tri - umph shall_ wave_

O'er the land_ of the free and the home of the brave?
O'er the land_ of the free and the home of the brave!
O'er the land_ of the free and the home of the brave!

Hurrah for the Flag

Words and music by John Philip Sousa

Hur - rah   for the   flag   of the   free, _____

May it   wave   as   our   stand - ard   for - ev - er,

The   gem   of the   land   and the   sea, _____

The ___   ban - ner   of   the   right. _____

Let   des - pots   re - mem - ber   the   day _____

When our   fa - thers   with   might - y   en - deav - or

Pro - claimed   as   they   marched   to   the   fray _____

That by   their   might   and   by   their   right   It   waves   for - ev - er!

John Philip Sousa is well known for his marches. One of his best-known marches is "Stars and Stripes Forever." Like many marches, this march has three sections. Sousa wrote words for the third part of the march, which is called the **trio**. The words and the melody of the two are found in the song "Hurrah for the Flag," p. 262.

Courtesy of The Peale Museum, Baltimore.

This painting illustrates the event in history which inspired the creation of "The Star-Spangled Banner": Francis Scott Key gazing at the flag through the morning mist. The artist planned his picture so that attention was focused on Key and then on the waving flag in the background. The strong dark and light contrast of the foreground figures and the rigging lines seem to make an almost perfect frame for the subtle colors of the background, including the flag.

Paint a picture of an important historical or current event that interests you. Your composition does not need to picture the event realistically. You may try to convey the ideas or beliefs underlying the incident or the feelings it aroused in you.

One day in 1893, Katherine Lee Bates, a professor of English from Massachusetts, visited Pike's Peak, Colorado. She was so impressed by the beauty around her that she wrote the poem "America, the Beautiful." After her poem was published, various people wrote melodies for it. Samuel Ward's stirring version is the one that is most familiar to us.

America, the Beautiful

Music *by* Samuel Ward
Words *by* Katharine Lee Bates
Arranged by Mary Val Marsh

1. O   beau - ti - ful   for   spa - cious skies,   For   am - ber   waves of   grain.
2. O   beau - ti - ful   for   pil - grim feet, Whose stern, im - pass-ion'd stress
3. O   beau - ti - ful   for   he - roes proved   In   lib - er - a - ting strife,
4. O   beau - ti - ful   for   pa - triot dream That sees   be - yond the   years,

For   pur - ple   moun-tain maj - es - ties,   A - bove the   fruit - ed   plain,
A   thor - ough-fare   for   free - dom beat   A - cross the   wil - der - ness.
Who more than self   their coun - try loved, And   mer - cy   more than life.
Thine al - a - bas - ter   cit - ies gleam Un - dim'd by   hu - man tears.

America! America! God shed his grace on thee,
America! America! God mend thine ev-'ry flaw,
America! America! May God, thy gold re-fine,
America! America! God shed His grace on thee,

A - mer - i - ca! A - mer - i - ca!

And crown thy good with broth-er-hood, From sea to shin-ing sea.
Con - firm thy soul in self con-trol, Thy lib-er-ty in law.
Till all suc-cess be no-ble-ness, And ev-'ry gain di-vine.
And crown thy good with broth-er-hood, From sea to shin-ing sea.

And crown thy good From sea to shin-ing sea.
Con - firm thy soul, Thy lib-er-ty in law.
Till no - ble-ness, And ev-'ry gain di-vine.
And crown thy good From sea to shin-ing sea.

This song symbolizes the pride that the Irish feel for their country.

The Wearing of the Green

Irish National Song

Oh,__ Pad - dy dear, and did you hear the news that's go - ing round?
Saint_ Pat - rick's Day no more we'll keep, his col - ors can't be seen,

The__ sham-rock is for - bid by law to grow on Ir - ish ground;
For__ there's a cru - el law a-gainst the wear - ing of the green.

I___ met with Nap-per Tan - dy and he took me by the hand,

And he said, "How's poor old Ire - land, and how___ does she stand?"

She's the most dis-tress-ful coun - try that ev - er yet was seen,

They are hang-ing men and wo - men for the wear - ing of the green.

Spring

Now Is the Month of Maying

Music by Thomas Morley

1. Now is the month of May - ing! When mer - ry lads are play - ing,
2. The Spring all clad in glad - ness Doth laugh at win - ter's sad - ness,

Fa la la la la la la la la, Fa la la la la la la!

Each with his bon - ny lass, A - danc - ing on the grass.
And to the bag - pipe's sound, The nymphs tread out their ground.

Fa la la la la!

Fa la la la la la la, Fa la la la la la.

Song On May Morning
(excerpt)

Hail, bounteous May, that dost inspire
Mirth, and youth, and warm desire!
Woods and groves are of thy dressing;
Hill and dale doth boast thy blessing.
Thus we salute thee with our early song,
And welcome thee, and wish thee long.

John Milton

Summer's Coming

Danish Round

1. Sum - mer's com - ing, sum - mer's com - ing, Sun and rain and
2. laugh-ter and song, Sun___ and___ rain and___
3.
4. laugh - ter, Ha ha ha! Laugh - ter, sun and song.

More Choral Music

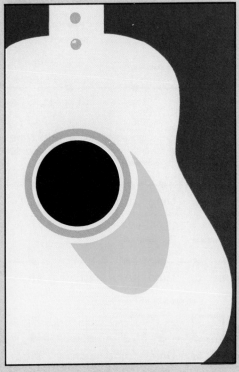

Playing the Guitar

What a Time for Music!

Carroll Rinehart

In marching tempo

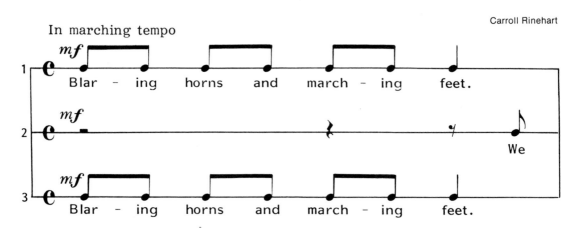

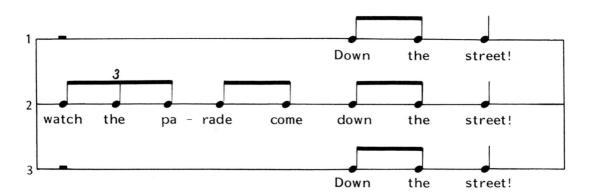

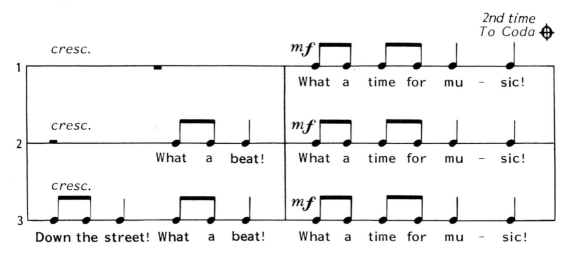

1, 2, 3, 4.

1 and 2 and 3 and 4.

Count-ing while they read the score.

Count-ing ev-er-more! Up and down the scales they go,

Count-ing ev-er-more! Scales they go,

ev-er-more! Down the scales they go,

pic-co-lo, Ev-'ry-one plays! What a show!

trum-pet, Then ev-'ry-one plays! What a show!

tu-ba, Ev-'ry-one plays! What a show!

D. C.

Coda

What a won-der-ful time for for mu-sic!

What a time for for mu-sic!

What a won-der-ful time for mu-sic! for mu-sic!

Buy Me Chocolate

George Mysels (A.S.C.A.P.)
Arranged by Hawley Ades

Moderate Calypso Tempo
Maracas

(Percussion continue these patterns until last four measures.)

mf All voices unison

Claves

1. A la-dy down in
2. At last she took them

San-ta Fe___ Took a walk to town one day.___ All her chil-dren
home a-gain;___ Put them all to bed, but then,___ Not a one would

tagged a-long,___ And as she walked you'd hear this song:
close an eye;___ Soon all the kids be-gan to cry:

1. Divide into 5 groups.

2. Groups 1 through 4 should sing their parts, once through, in order.

3. When completed, begin again with Group 1 and add each part in cumulative fashion until Group 5 has sung the following four lines:

"Chil-dren, you're driv-ing me cra-zy!"
"Chil-dren, I have-n't the mon-ey!"
"Chil-dren, your pa-pa's not work-ing!"
"Chil-dren, why can't you be qui-et!"

4. Sing Verse 2 in unison. Then repeat the above.

5. Go on to the next page.

Group 1 *p* with childlike whine   *D.C.*

"Ma - ma, buy me choc-o-late!"
(2) bring

Group 2 *mp* more insistent   *D.C.*

"Ma - ma buy_ me some lem-on-ade!"
(2) bring

Group 3 *mf* demanding   *D.C.*

"Ma - ma, buy me cook-ies!"
(2) bring

Group 4 *f* forcefully   *D.C.*

"Buy me some pea - nuts!"
(2) "Bring

Group 5 *ff*   ⎡—3—⎤   *D.C.*

("Chil - dren, you're driv-ing me cra - zy!")

272

273

The Colorado Trail

American Folk Song
Words and Music adapted by Lee Hays
Arranged by Marilyn Rinehart

Slow and dreamy (♩ = 66)

1. Eyes like a morn-ing star, Cheek like a rose,
2. Stars fad-ing up a-bove, Lark starts to sing,

Ah____ Ah____

Lau-ra was a pret-ty girl, Ev-'ry-bod-y knows.
Sky is ros-y in the east, What will this day bring?

Ah____

Weep all ye lit-tle rains, wail, winds,— wail.

Ah____ Ah____

All a-long, a-long, a-long the Col-o-rad-o Trail.

Ah____

3. Eyes like a prai-rie flow'r, Laugh-ing all the day.

Oo____

Lau-ra was a love-ly girl, Now she's gone a-way.

Weep ye rains, Wail, winds, wail.

Weep all ye lit-tle rains, Wail, winds,_ wail.

All a-long, a-long, a - long the trail.

All a-long, a-long, a-long the Col-o-rad-o Trail.

Oo____

Oo____

Promised Land

Natalie Sleeth

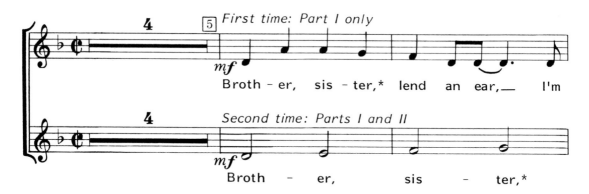

* Alternate: "Sister, brother," "All you children," "All you sisters (brothers)."

O, chil-dren,* won't you rise and fol-low, one and all? Bet-ter days are now in___ view,___ I'm head-in' for the prom-ised land! All my dreams are com-in'___ true,___ I'm head-in' for the prom-ised land! Want to leave the past be-hind,___

O, chil-dren,* won't you rise and fol-low, one and all? Bet - ter days are now in view, and all the dreams I dreamed are com - in' true! I'll leave the past be - hind and

Alternate: sisters, brothers.

face the fu-ture with a hope-ful mind,— Peace and joy I'll

keep a hope-ful mind for joy I'll

sure-ly— find,— I'm head-in' for the prom-ised

find, I'm head-in' for the prom-ised

1.
land!
2. *mp*
land! Head-in' for the prom-ised land!

2. *mp*
land! Head-in' for the prom-ised land!

65 *f*
Head-in' for the prom-ised land!_____ *(whispered):* yeah!

f
Head-in' for the prom-ised land!_____ *(whispered):* yeah!

*Optional

Alleluia

Michael Praetorius
Arrangement by Maurice Gardner

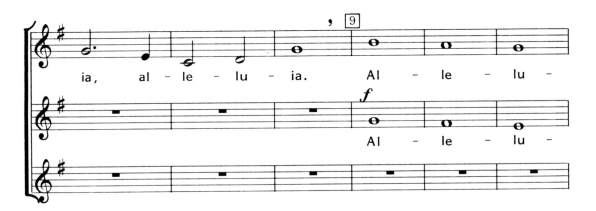

Earthsounds

Words and Music by Jane Allen
Arr. by Carroll Rinehart and Herbert Allen

283

bees?_____   Or can you hear the sigh-ing of the
way?_____   Lis - ten to the ea - gle's call,___

bees?_____   Or can you hear the sigh-ing of the
way?_____   Lis - ten to the ea - gle's call,___

dim.

wind, the o-cean's roar,   Or do you hear your neigh-bor
fly - ing free and wild,   Or hear the lone - ly cry-ing

dim.

wind, the o-cean's roar,___   Or do you hear your neigh-bor
fly - ing free and wild,___   Or hear the lone - ly cry-ing

(v. 1) *knock knock*

unis.

knock-ing at_your door?
of a hun-gry child?   Sounds of joy_   or

sounds of pain,   Sum-mer sun_   or wind and rain,

cresc.

Songs of peace_   or sounds of war,   Voi-ces new   or

PLAYING THE GUITAR
AND THE BARITONE UKULELE

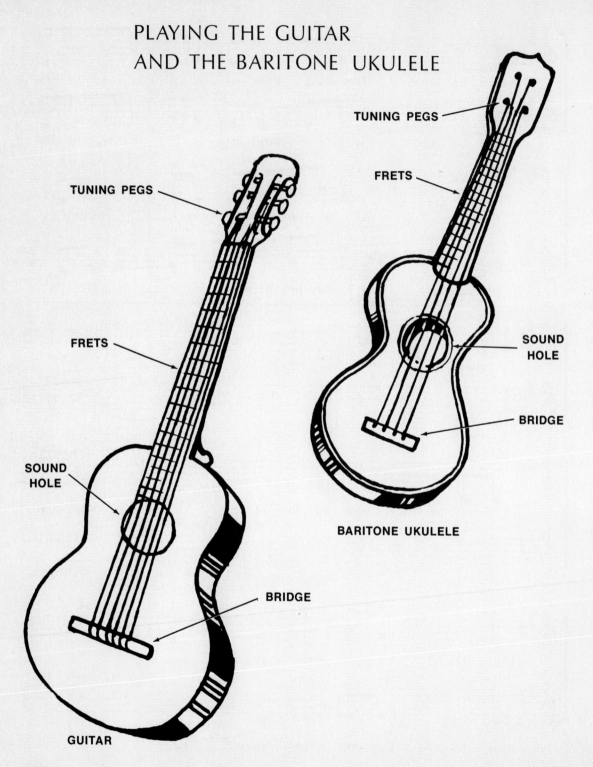

TUNING PEGS

FRETS

SOUND HOLE

BRIDGE

BARITONE UKULELE

TUNING PEGS

FRETS

SOUND HOLE

BRIDGE

GUITAR

The guitar and the baritone ukulele have similar shapes, but the guitar is the larger of the two. Because the tuning of the guitar and the baritone ukulele are very similar, you can use the same fingerings for both instruments. The tenor guitar has the same tuning as the baritone ukulele; therefore, the fingerings for these two are the same.

The strings of the guitar are tuned to these pitches.

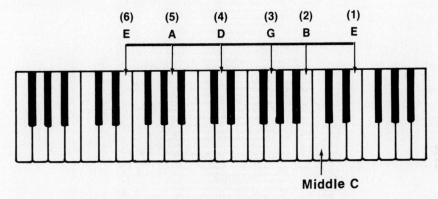

The tuning for the baritone ukulele and tenor guitar is the same as that of the first four strings of the guitar.

(4)	(3)	(2)	(1)
D	G	B	E

Form a C shape with the thumb and fingers of your left hand. Slip the neck of the guitar between these fingers, with the thumb of the left hand behind the neck of the guitar. Keep the thumb and fingers relaxed so that your fingers can move easily when you change chords.

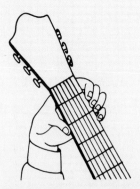

The following numbers on the fingering charts, or **tablatures,** are used to indicate which fingers should be used.

1 — index finger
2 — middle finger
3 — ring finger
4 — little finger

The right hand is used for strumming or plucking the guitar. The strings may be strummed with the thumb, or the thumb may be used to pluck the lower strings. The first, second, and third fingers are used to pluck the upper strings.

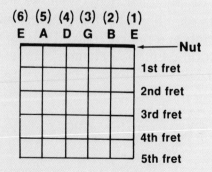

Tablatures show the strings and **frets** of the instruments. The frets are the raised metal strips on the neck; they are shown on the tablature by horizontal lines. The strings are shown by vertical lines.

(6)	(5)	(4)	(3)	(2)	(1)
E	A	D	G	B	E

← Nut
1st fret
2nd fret
3rd fret
4th fret
5th fret

The songs in this book that can be played on the guitar are indicated by tablatures above the melody.

TUNING YOUR GUITAR

The easiest way to tune your instrument is to adjust each string so that it will be in tune with another string. Follow these steps.

1. Play the E two octaves below middle C on the piano. Adjust the low E string (the sixth string) by turning the tuning peg until you reach the correct pitch.

2. Place your finger between the fourth and fifth frets on the E string. Pluck this string and you will hear the note A. Adjust the A string (the fifth string) until the two pitches sound the same.

3. Place your finger between the fourth and fifth frets on the A string (fifth string) and adjust the D string (fourth string) until the two pitches sound the same.

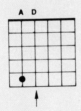

4. Place your finger between the fourth and fifth frets on the D string (fourth string) and tune the G string (third string) until the two pitches sound the same.

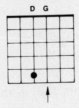

5. Place your finger between the third and fourth frets on the G string (third string) and tune the B string (second string) until the two pitches sound the same.

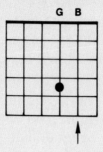

6. Place your finger between the fourth and fifth frets on the B string (second string) and tune the high E string (first string) until the two pitches sound the same.

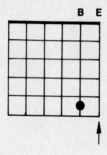

Here is the tablature for the D major chord.

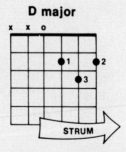

The black dots show you where to place your fingers. The circle means to strum the **open** (unfingered) string. No part of your hand should touch an open string. A string marked with an "X" indicates that the string is not to be played.

The D major chord:

1. Place the second finger on the first string between the first and second frets.
2. Place the third finger on the second string, between the second and third frets.
3. Place the first finger on the third string, between the first and second frets.

Strum only the first four strings of the guitar. This is the D major chord.

Practice strumming:

Strum the D on each strong pulse to accompany "Row, Row, Row Your Boat."

Row, Row, Row Your Boat

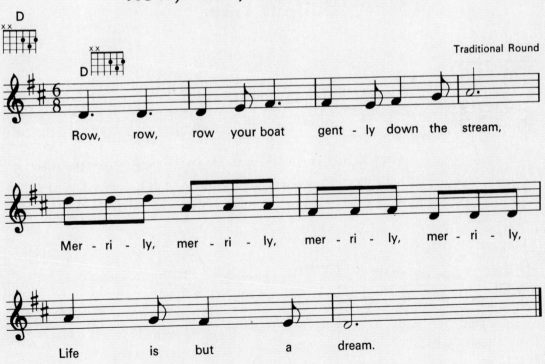

Traditional Round

Row, row, row your boat gent - ly down the stream,

Mer - ri - ly, mer - ri - ly, mer - ri - ly, mer - ri - ly,

Life is but a dream.

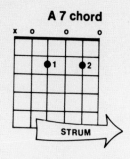

A 7 chord

The A7 chord:

1. Place your second finger on the second string, between the first and second frets.
2. Place your first finger on the fourth string, between the first and second frets.
3. Strum across the first five strings only.

Both the A7 chord and the D chord are needed to accompany "Buffalo Gals." Strum twice per measure.

Buffalo Gals

Traditional

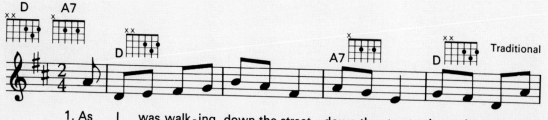

1. As I was walk-ing down the street, down the street, down the street, A
2. I asked her if she'd stop and talk, stop and talk, stop and talk, Her

pret-ty gal I chanced to meet, oh she was fair to see.
feet took up the whole side-walk, and left no room for me.

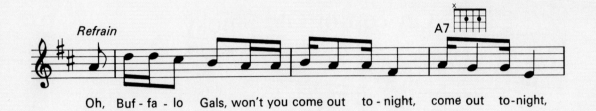

Refrain

Oh, Buf - fa - lo   Gals, won't you come out   to - night,   come out   to - night,

come out   to - night? Oh, Buf - fa - lo   Gals, won't you come out   to - night, and

dance   by   the   light   of   the   moon?

The G major chord:

1. Place the third finger on the first string, between the second and third frets.
2. Place the first finger on the fifth string, between the first and second frets.
3. Place the second finger on the sixth string, between the second and third frets.
4. Strum all six strings.

The D, G, and A7 chords are needed to play "On Top of Old Smoky." Strum once per measure.

Practice strumming:

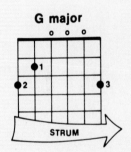

G major

STRUM

On Top of Old Smoky

American Folk Song

1. On top of old Smok-y_____ all cov-ered with snow,_____
2. Oh, court-ing's a pleas-ure_____ and part-ing is grief,_____
3. A thief will but rob you_____ and take what you save,_____

I lost my true lov-er_____ by_ court-ing too slow._____
And a false heart-ed lov-er_____ is_ worse than a thief._____
But a false heart-ed lov-er_____ will_ lead to the grave._____

The D, G, and A7 chords are used in "Camptown Races." Review the three chords to be sure you know the fingerings. Accompany the song. How many times per measure will you strum?

Camptown Races

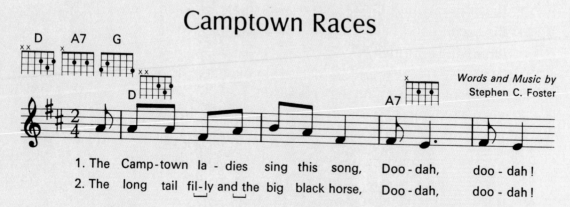

Words and Music by
Stephen C. Foster

1. The Camp-town la - dies sing this song, Doo - dah, doo - dah!
2. The long tail fil-ly and the big black horse, Doo - dah, doo - dah!

The Camp-town race track five miles long, Oh, doo - dah - day.
They flew the track and both cut a-cross, Oh, doo - dah - day.

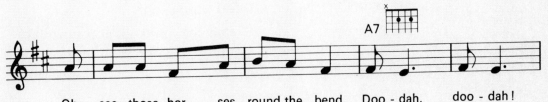

Oh, see those hor - ses round the bend, Doo - dah, doo - dah!
The blind horse stick-ing in a big mud hole, Doo - dah, doo - dah!

Guess that race will nev - er end, Oh, doo - dah - day.
Could-n't touch bot-tom with a ten - foot pole, Oh, doo - dah - day.

Goin' to run all night, goin' to run all day. I'll bet my mon-ey on the

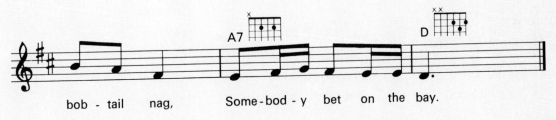

bob - tail nag, Some-bod - y bet on the bay.

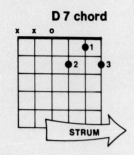

D 7 chord

x x o

STRUM

The D7 chord:

1. Place your third finger on the first string, between the first and second frets.
2. Place your first finger on the second string, between the nut and the first fret.
3. Place your second finger on the third string, between the first and second frets.
4. Strum across the first four strings only.

The G and D7 chords may be used to accompany "Polly Wolly Doodle." Strum twice for each measure. Practice strumming:

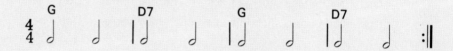

Polly Wolly Doodle

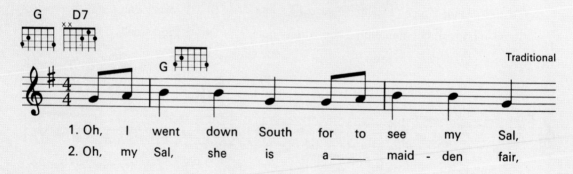

Traditional

1. Oh, I went down South for to see my Sal,
2. Oh, my Sal, she is a_____ maid - den fair,

Sing - ing Pol - ly Wol - ly Doo - dle all the day;
Sing - ing Pol - ly Wol - ly Doo - dle all the day;

My ___ Sal, she is a spunk-y gal,
With ___ cur-ly eyes and laugh-ing hair,

Sing-ing Pol-ly Wol-ly Doo-dle all the day.
Sing-ing Pol-ly Wol-ly Doo-dle all the day.

Refrain

Fare thee well, fare thee well, Fare thee well, my fair-y fay,

For I'm goin' to Loui-si-an-a, for to see my Su-sy-an-na,

Sing-ing Pol-ly Wol-ly Doo-dle all the day.

3. Behind the barn down on my knees,
   Singing Polly Wolly Doodle all the day;
   I thought I heard a chicken sneeze,
   Singing Polly Wolly Doodle all the day.
   Refrain

4. He sneezed so hard with the whooping cough,
   Singing Polly Wolly Doodle all the day;
   He sneezed his head and tail right off,
   Singing Polly Wolly Doodle all the day.
   Refrain

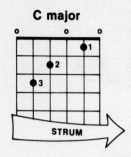

C major

STRUM

The C major chord:

1. Place your first finger on the second string, between the nut and the first fret.

2. Place your second finger on the fourth string, between the first and second frets.

3. Place your third finger on the fifth string, between the second and third frets.

4. Strum all six strings.

Practice the G, C, and D7 chords before you accompany "Old Dan Tucker."

Practice strumming:

Old Dan Tucker

Words and Music by
Dan Emmett

1. I came to town the oth-er night, I heard the noise and
2. Old Dan Tuck-er was a fine old man, he washed his face in the

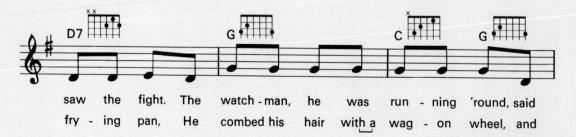

saw the fight. The watch-man, he was run-ning 'round, said
fry-ing pan, He combed his hair with a wag-on wheel, and

"Old Dan Tuck-er's come to town."
died with a tooth-ache in his heel.
Get out the way, old Dan Tuck-er, Get out the way, old Dan Tuck-er, Get out the way, old Dan Tuck-er. You're too late to come to sup-per.

3. Now, old Dan Tucker and I fell out,
and what do you think it was all about?
He borrowed my old setting hen
and didn't bring her back again.
Refrain

4. Now old Dan Tucker, he came to town
to swing the ladies all around,
Swing them right and swing them left
then to the one he liked the best.
Refrain

Other songs which may be accompanied with the G, C, and D7 chords are "Fender Bender," page 5 and "The Cowboy," page 24.

Strumming

After you have had some practice with strumming and changing chords, you may want to experiment with new ways of strumming. Using different strums will give variety to your accompaniments.

1. You have been using the **basic strum,** a downward stroke with the side of the thumb. For most songs, a strum on the strong pulse of the music is appropriate. If the tempo is very slow, you may want to strum on every beat.

2. You can vary the basic strum by brushing the lowest-pitched string of the chord with your thumb, and then brushing the other strings with your fingers on the next beat. Try strumming a D major chord in this way.

thumb brush thumb brush thumb brush thumb brush

3. Here is another simple strum:
   a. Use the thumb to pluck the lowest note of the chord.
   b. Use the first three fingers to pluck the first three strings. Pluck all three strings at once. Pluck the third string with your first finger, the second string with your second finger, and the first string with your third finger.
   c. The movement of the fingers should be *upwards* (toward the player).

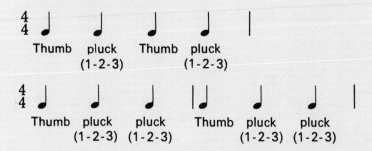

4. You may enjoy experimenting with other strums. Try plucking the strings individually in **arpeggio** (broken chord) patterns. In an arpeggio, the notes are sounded individually rather than together.

CHORD CHARTS

The following chord charts will provide a handy guide for reviewing chord fingerings. They will also be helpful in learning to play new chords.

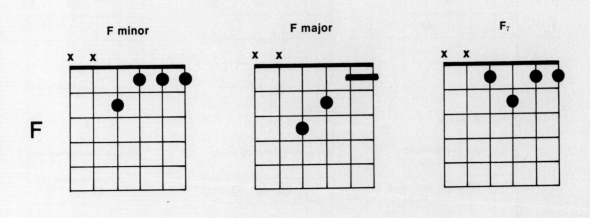

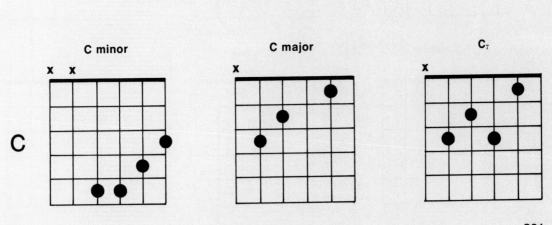

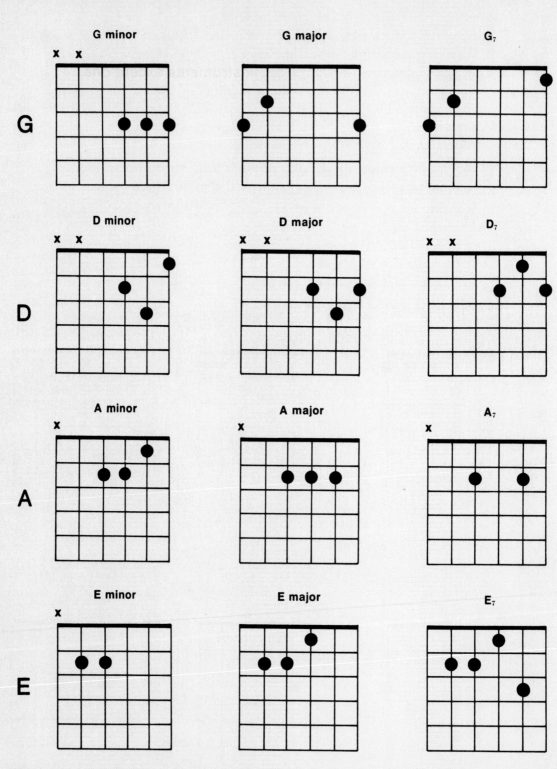

Do You Know?

1. All the following are stringed instruments except one. Which is it?

   banjo   koto   balalaika   timpani   dulcimer

2. The lute, unlike the flute, is a stringed instrument that is somewhat like a guitar. Is this statement true or false?

3. Although there are many kinds of rock music, all of them have one thing in common. What is it?

4. Here are some rhythm patterns. Two are common in rock music. Which one would be found least often in rock music?

- Here is the first line of the song "He's Got the Whole World in His Hands." Sing the line or listen to it on the recording of the song. Then answer questions 5–9 about this music.

1. He's got the whole world in His hands,
2. He's got the wind and rain in His hands,

1. He's got the whole wide world, He's got the whole wide world,
2. He's got the wind and rain, He's got the wind and rain,

5. How many different voice parts are shown in the music?

6. Look at the top staff of the music. What is the most used interval? What other interval is used on this staff?

7. On the top staff what kind of rhythm occurs on the words "whole world" and "in his hands?"

8. Reading from the lower staff to the upper staff what are the notes that begin the first full measure? These notes form a chord. What is the root of the chord? What is the name of the chord?

9. This is a religious song originated by Afro-Americans who lived during the days of slavery. What is such a song called?

10. Which one of the Listening Selections in this book did you enjoy hearing most? What kind of music is it? Tell what you liked about it.

• Here is the beginning of the song "Simple Gifts." Questions 11–15 are about this music.

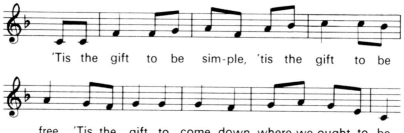

'Tis the gift to be sim-ple, 'tis the gift to be

free, 'Tis the gift to come down where we ought to be,

11. Notice that the meter signature is missing in the music above. Look at the values of the notes in each measure and write the correct meter signature on your answer sheet.

12. How slow or fast do you want the song to be sung? Write in a tempo marking you think would be suitable.

13. Should the music be played softly or loudly or in between? Write in the dynamic markings you think the music should have.

14. Should the music get louder or softer at any point? If you think it should, add the proper symbols.

15. Now sing the song yourself or with a group of classmates. Be sure to observe the markings you have added to the song. Compare the way you have interpreted it with the interpretations of others in the class. Make a list of the ways in which they differ or are the same.

For Fun

THE STORY OF FRITZ HEINRICH BUBERT

Fritz Bubert was a young man of sixteen when he decided to become a famous composer. He had never studied music, but he felt that he had a good ear, and he loved to strum his ukulele as he hummed arias from the great operas.

One day Fritz's opportunity arrived. He received in the mail a notice of a contest for composers. A music publisher was offering a large sum of money as a prize for the best composition.

Quickly Fritz went to his desk to get pen and paper. Very carefully he drew music staves all the way down the sheet, and then drew treble clef signs at the beginning of each line. He decided to have a meter of three, so he wrote in the meter signature $\frac{3}{6}$. He then added the key signature of two flats for the key of D minor. Now he was ready to add the notes of his melody.

Fritz scribbled notes all over the page and then added two more pages to his composition. He marked the first phrase *crescendo* so the players would remember to play softly, and at the very end he wrote *pianissimo* so the music would end with a loud crash. To add variety he marked *pizzicato* in one section for the flutes, and in one place where the drums entered, he marked a careful *legato* to make sure the drummer accented each sound.

When Fritz had finished, he re-read his composition carefully, making sure that each staff had six lines and that the horizontal bars were drawn correctly. He put his title at the very top of the music—*Sonata For Tuba and Orchestra.* Then he put his composition in an envelope and mailed it to the publisher.

Poor Fritz! Two weeks later his composition was returned with a short note:

Dear Mr. Bubu:

We strongly recommend that you attend a good music school before sending us any more manuscripts.

Very truly yours,

The Publisher

Why do you think the publisher did not accept Fritz's manuscript? Find at least ten reasons.

COMPOSER'S CORNER

This is a project to work on by yourself.

You need staff paper, a pencil, and resonator bells or piano.

You might want to work on different days, for a few minutes at a time.

Write your own music:

Make up a musical motif, using five different pitches. (Use the pitches C D E G A in any order or select your own group of pitches.) Write this musical motif in whole notes on the staff. (Here is our musical motif, just for an example.)

Decide upon a meter—$\frac{3}{4}$, $\frac{4}{4}$, $\frac{6}{8}$ or even $\frac{7}{8}$.

Begin your composition with your musical motif. Use some eighth notes and some quarter notes to make your rhythm more interesting.

Repeat some of the notes in your motif. Vary your motif. Use your motif more than once; use some different notes. Listen to what you have written and make changes if you think they are needed. Make your melody at least four measures long.

If you have trouble beginning, you might:

Use the rhythm of one of the songs in the book, but write different pitches.

Use the pitches in one of the songs in the book, but change the meter and the length of each note.

Play your composition for others.

Say It with Movement

CIRCLE DANCES

Circle dances have been popular in many parts of the world. It is thought by some that the earliest dances done by primitive people were in closed circle formation, to symbolize tribal unity. Circle dances are most popular today in the Balkan nations, although they are danced in other countries as well.

You may know the hora, considered to be the national dance of Israel. The hora probably originated in Rumania. You can dance the hora to both "Kuma Echa," p. 80, and "Tzena, Tzena," p. 132.

Here are the directions for a more complex dance to "Kuma Echa." You will need to walk through and practice each part of the dance before you can put it all together with the music.

FORMATION: Circle without partners, all facing center with hands joined.

MEASURE 1: Take 3 small running steps toward the center, starting with the Right foot (Right, Left, Right, and hop on the Right). Everyone should lean forward slightly, raising head and arms while going forward.

MEASURE 2: Reverse direction, moving backward (Left, Right, Left, and hop on the Left.) Arms are lowered while moving backward.

MEASURE 3: Do a "grapevine" step to the left. (Cross Right foot over the Left and place weight on it, move Left foot to the left and step on it, step with Right foot behind Left, taking a small leap onto the Left foot.

MEASURE 4: Repeat grapevine step.

MEASURES 5–8: Repeat measures 1–4

Learn this much of the dance well before proceeding. You can dance these two steps to the whole song. When you are ready to learn the rest of the dance, here are the directions:

MEASURE 9: The circle moves toward the right, as you take 4 short running steps. (Facing right, run Right and Left; then, twisting your body to the left, run backwards *in the same direction,* Right and Left.)

MEASURES 10–12: Continue the running step, three times more.

MEASURE 13: Run forward toward center with 4 steps (Right, Left, Right, Left.)

MEASURE 14: Move backward slowly by stamping once on the Right foot and placing the Left foot beside it. On the Right-foot stamp, lean forward and push hands forward; on the Left-foot step, straighten up.

MEASURES 15–16: Repeat measure 14 twice.

Use some of the steps you have learned for "Kuma Echa" to make up a dance for "Tzena, Tzena."

CREATING IMAGES THROUGH MOVEMENT

Feelings and ideas can be expressed through movement as well as through words. Without using words, try to say the following things to another person:

"Hello!"

"Go away!"

"I like that."

"No, no, stop!"

What parts of your body did you use to express each idea?

Your face? Head?   Fingers? Hands? Arms?

Shoulders? Torso?   Legs? Feet?

Choose one of the four ideas, and try it again. How well did you express your idea this time?

The ideas in poetry can often be expressed through movement. Read the poem, "On Watching the Construction of a Skyscraper," on p. 168. What are the images suggested by this poem? How could you express the ideas in the poem through movement?

Work with as many people as you need. When you have worked out your ideas, share them with others. How did your ideas differ from theirs?

Write or find other poems to interpret through movement.

GLOSSARY OF TERMS

altered tones—changes in some of the pitches of a melody, **143**

antiphonal—music in which one group of voices or instruments answers another group, **44**

art song—a composition for solo voice and instrumental accompaniment (usually keyboard). The term "art song" is used to distinguish such songs from folk songs or popular songs, **232**

augmentation—doubling the duration of notes in a melody, **143**

balalaika—a triangular, guitar-like instrument, **31**

banjo—a stringed instrument having a long neck and a circular body covered with calfskin or parchment, **28**

body—a part of the guitar and other stringed instruments over which the strings are stretched, **22**

cadence—two or more chords which bring a line or a melody to a point of rest, **153**

chord—a combination of three or more tones sounded together, **120**

chord root—the letter name of a scale tone upon which a chord is built, **120**

console—the part of a pipe organ containing the keyboards and the stops, **53**

countermelody—a melody that is written to harmonize another melody, **118**

dulcimer—a stringed instrument having a hollow wooden body with metal strings stretched over a sounding board and played by plucking, **30**

duple meter—a meter that has two or four beats per measure, **9**

extension—notes added to a piece of music to lengthen it, **143**

finger board—the strip of wood in the neck of a guitar and other stringed instruments against which the strings are pressed with the fingers, **22**

flamenco music—a brilliant and colorful blend of Spanish and gypsy dance music, **23**

frets—small bars of metal or other material attached to the finger board of a guitar and other stringed instruments, **22**

interval—the distance between two tones, **120**

inversion—a change in the arrangement of the notes of a chord so that the root of the chord is not at the bottom, **123**

irregular meter—a measure with five, seven, or more odd numbers of beats, **72**

koto—a stringed instrument consisting of an oblong wooden body, usually with thirteen strings stretched over it, and played by plucking, **31**

light opera—see *operetta,* **186**

lute—a guitar-like instrument that has a fretted neck and round back, **26**

manuals—the keyboards of a pipe organ, **53**

melodic rhythm—the rhythm of a melody, **74**

meter—the grouping of beats within a measure, as indicated by the meter signature at the beginning of a composition, **66**

meter signature—numbers written on the staff at the beginning of a composition indicating the kind and number of counts or beats used in a measure, **66**

microtonal music—music based on intervals smaller than half steps, **110**

mode—a scale, **94**

motif—a short rhythmic or melodic pattern, **138**

nationalism—a strong sense of national pride often expressed through music, art, and literature, **226**

neck—a part of the guitar and other stringed instruments to which the finger board is attached, **22**

opera—a play told through acting, singing, and instrumental music, **186**

operetta—a light, often humorous opera, usually with spoken dialogue, **186**

ornamentation—new tones added to decorate a melody, **143**

pentatonic scale—a five-tone scale, **98**

phrase form—a way of building music by putting phrases together, often with one or two phrases repeated. This is a form that can be indicated by letters, such as A B, or A B A, **162**

pipe organ—a keyboard instrument which produces sounds by air being blown through pipes, **52**

pulse—a steady underlying beat that recurs throughout a piece of music, **64**

scale—a series of tones ascending or descending in pitch according to fixed intervals, **92**

symphony—an orchestral composition usually consisting of three or four movements, **183**

syncopation—the placing of accents on beats that are not normally stressed, **77**

synthesizer—an electronic device that can imitate the sounds of many musical instruments as well as non-musical sounds, **60**

tonal center—the first tone of the scale, **101**

tone row—a twelve-note scale with no tonal center, in which each pitch is of equal importance, **106**

treble—the high range of a child's voice, **40**

triad—a chord of three tones, consisting of a chord root plus the third and fifth above it, **120**

triple meter—meter in which the basic grouping of beats is divisible by three, **73**

triplet—a group of three notes of equal value that are played in the same amount of time that two of the same notes normally receive, **84**

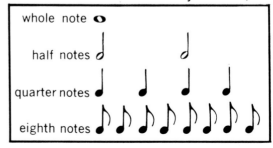

CLASSIFIED INDEX

LISTENING SELECTIONS

Symphony No. 94, Movements 2 and 4
(*F.J. Haydn*), **183**

Take Five
(*D. Brubeck*), **173**

Toccata in D minor
(*J.S. Bach*), **53**

Tum-Balalaika
(Russian Folk Song), **31**

Under the Apple Tree

(Russian Folk Song), **31**

Verdad
(Flamenco Guitar), **23**

Waltz
(*W. Russell*), **73**

Waltz in C# minor, Op. 64, No. 2
(*F. Chopin*), **232**

The Web
(*D. Ward-Steinman*), **109**

ALPHABETICAL SONG INDEX

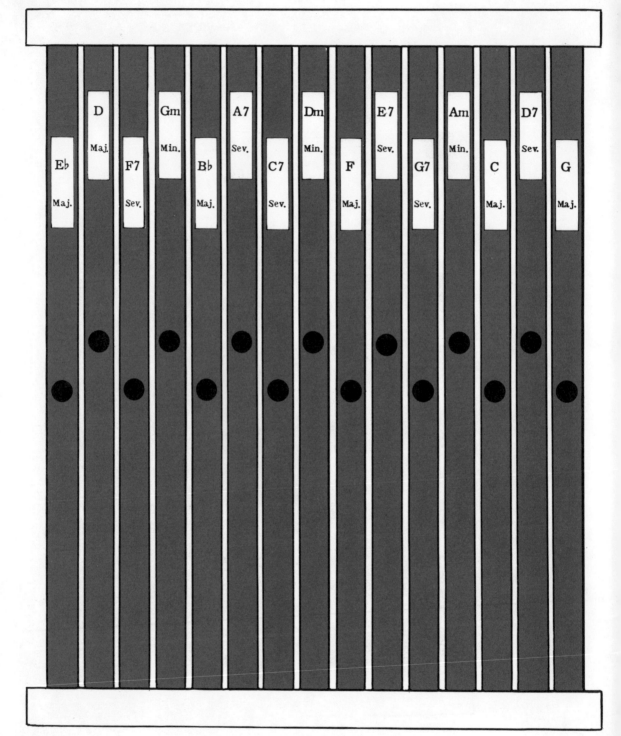